THE WINE
EXPLORER

THE WINE EXPLORER

Graham Mitchell

The University of Buckingham Press

First published in Great Britain in 2013 by
The University of Buckingham Press
51 Gower Street
London WC1E 6HJ

Reprinted with corrections in 2020

© The University of Buckingham Press, 2013, 2020

www.unibuckinghampress.com

CIP catalogue record for this book is available at the British Library

ISBN 9781789559378

For Nicola, Ned, Harry, Ella and Bea, with all my love.

The Author

"Graham is to wine what Michael Palin is to travel… a sort of Indiana Jones with a corkscrew."

Graham Mitchell has been buying and selling wine for twenty years as a professional wine merchant. Known as the "Wine Explorer", he noses his way around vineyards off the beaten track. He travels the world searching for the best wines, those with attitude and soul.

Graham is the fourth generation in his family to toil in wine. His great-grandfather, Sir Alfred Bower, established Bower and Company, wine merchants in the City of London in 1879, so you could say that wine is in his blood!

A Director of El Vino Company for six years, Graham subsequently followed his great grandfather's example and set up his own wine business. His wit and passion for wine led to a wine slot on BBC radio for eight years and much lecturing and writing about wine in the press. He has written for the *Telegraph* has regularly selected the Wine Explorer's wines for the *Spectator* magazine. He also has a reputation as one of the better after-dinner speakers in the UK, blending information with humour and thus leading his audience on an entertaining journey through the vineyards of the world.

He started his career packing cases in the cellar at Berry Bros and Rudd. In 1983 he spent six back-breaking weeks picking grapes at Château Angludet in Bordeaux. He has also worked in the Mosel Valley in Germany, analysing the chemical constituents of wine. He has travelled widely the vineyards of the world, including buying visits to

France, Germany, Portugal, Australia, New Zealand, Argentina, Chile, California, British Columbia and South Africa.

Graham lives with his wife Nicola, four children, Ned, Harry, Ella and Bea, and Clemmie the dog in, er, tranquil Warwickshire.

The Wine Explorer – in a glass of his own

And if you really want to get behind the label:
Web: www.thewineexplorer.co.uk/
Twitter: twitter.com/thewineexplorer
Email: graham@thewineexplorer.co.uk

Acknowledgements

My thanks must firstly go to my father for introducing me to wine and for his encouragement and initial grounding in this fascinating world.

Thank you to Henry Blofeld for his well-chosen and, as ever, cultured words in the Foreword.

I am delighted to include pen-and-ink drawings by my late mother Pamela and my niece Lizzie Fane, for which I am mightily grateful. I also want to thank Andy Hayward, who badgered me to write this book and whose advice was invaluable. Errors and omissions are all mine, as are all the opinions.

Thank you to Christopher Woodhead and James Wickham, the publishers of the first edition, for showing such faith in me and having the imagination to see the potential of this book.

Foreword by Henry Blofeld

I think I am probably in almost anyone's first eleven for my enjoyment of wine, but when it comes to the question of knowledge about what I am drinking and where it comes from, I am well at the back of the also-rans. Graham Mitchell's charming book, taking us around the world of wine and bringing it delightfully to life through his own personal adventures, will, I hope, allow me to climb a place or two in this particular batting order.

Graham and I both have a great love of wine, but there the similarities end. He is a top-end expert at it all; I am a low-end slurper. Having read his book, I shall now do all I can to stagger round as many of the exciting wine-producing parts of the world he has told us all about – and with his book ready at hand. He gives us the flavour of the wine and, just as important, the flavour of the country, which makes it all more fun and rounds off the story so well.

We lurch in taxis driven by Miguel, on journeys with a gaucho called Jesus; we eat flame-grilled beef in the Pampas; we climb Mount Kilimanjaro (and a pyramid or two, but in a non-vinous part of the world). We eat at the brilliant Reubens restaurant in Franschhoek – I have done this too, and can vouch for it; we learn that baboons and Cape cobras have a discouraging effect on the process of growing grapes; and so much more besides. I laughed aloud.

All the major grape varieties are present in their most mouth-watering forms, and most of the serious wine-producing parts of the world. We even have an amusing, but perhaps superfluous, chapter on whether or not wine is good for you and what should be a suitable daily intake. I would have thought this is not a subject that winemakers or wine merchants would normally be wise to tackle. But Graham skates through it beautifully, reminding us that more than three hundred doctors have become winemakers. And that the best definition of an alcoholic is… well, I'll leave you to find out the answer to that one.

It is a splendid book, which will, I fear, lead me in only one direction, and that is not towards abstinence. Great value, great fun, highly instructive and informative, deliciously amusing and written with a refreshing innocence and none of the pompous or patronising diktats to be found in many wine books. I can think of nothing that I would like to receive more as a Christmas present. Well done Graham, take a bow.

Henry Blofeld

Contents

"There was this wonderful view set in a blameless blue sky… we were chatting about cricket, the wine was twinkling in my glass and I just thought I'd died and gone to heaven."
Sir Trevor McDonald

Like Cyrano de Bergerac, my nose normally arrives at a vineyard about fifteen minutes before the rest of me. I am an explorer, and a wine explorer needs a good nose to sniff out the best and most exquisitely crafted wines in the world. That's my job: I buy and sell wine for a living. It would appear, however, that my job description isn't understood by everyone. I was rather taken aback when a few years ago I arrived at my 11-year-old son Harry's school to be met by one of his teachers who said, *"Ah, Mr Mitchell, I gather from your son that you're a drug dealer – how's business?"*

1

I'd like you to follow my adventures so I can reveal the inside track to you, the intriguing world behind the labels, so that you can accompany me on a light-hearted journey through the most interesting vineyards on earth. I want to share some remarkable stories, copious humorous anecdotes and uncork some of my discoveries with you.

There is something rather beguiling about the juice of the vine which attracts perfectly sane people into this hazardous and impecunious industry. It's hard work, often physically demanding, with limited return, but there is also an enchantment, excitement and enduring appeal which makes it all worthwhile... most of the time. A miraculous alchemy takes place when a bottle of wine is opened and shared. I suppose you could say that water divides the nations of the world, but wine unites them. It's not just that the vineyards seem to be located in some of the most naturally beautiful territories of the world, surrounded by outrageously fabulous restaurants, where local food and wine join together in a sumptuous embrace; it's something else, it's something intangible, dreamy and irresistible. One of my Bordeaux suppliers once remarked to me that he didn't really sell wine, he sold *dreams*.

I know what he means. Sometimes I am emailed by people who have visited one of the vineyards abroad which I represent in the UK. There was a couple who were married at a vineyard called the Red Hill Estate on the magical Mornington Peninsula, south of Melbourne in Australia; memories and daydreams of that special occasion could be revisited by opening a bottle from that same vineyard, possibly from the same vintage as their visit, and whilst drinking they could feed on the memories evoked *in vino veritas*. There is a truth in the beauty of an experience, if Keats will forgive me for saying so.

Sometimes wine can enable us to remember and relive that experience and dream that dream again. I remember a few years ago I visited the Napa Valley with my wife. We took Ned, our eldest son, who was six months old at the time, around the wineries in a backpack before leaving to spend a couple of days in Yosemite National Park. The last vineyard we visited was called Frog's Leap, and I spent two hours being shown around and tasting the wines from this organic winery in Napa. The wines are elegant and restrained – certainly more subtle than many of the wines from this region – but marketed brilliantly by the owner, John Williams. While we tasted the wines he told me of the evening he spent with some friends, sitting around the fire with a beer, trying to decide what to call the vineyard, when a frog leapt out of the undergrowth nearby and hopped across his line of vision. The decision was made! I bought a couple of bottles from John to fortify us on our onward journey. When we arrived at the little log cabin in Yosemite it was freezing; snow had fallen recently. Darkness descended, and, having put Ned to bed, Nicola and I sat in front of a blazing log fire with a bottle of Frog's Leap Zinfandel, poured into a jug sitting by the fire, gradually warming. It was a magical evening; we talked and talked, and sipped and sipped, and this wine was just magnificent. It had the most beautiful balance of ripe fruit and subtle oak; as it "breathed" it was developing complexity, and served at warmish room temperature, it was silky and seductive – just breathtaking. The wine had so many stories to tell, and so did I. If I am ever lucky enough to taste a bottle from the Frog's Leap winery today – and these wines are not inexpensive – I always remember that special evening in Yosemite, and it is the wine that brings those memories flooding back.

Unfortunately, a considerable amount of wine imported into the UK is incredibly dull. Much wine lacks character, is bland and blended for the mass-market volume brands, mainly sold off the shelf and massively discounted in a supermarket or big retail chain. These concoctions increasingly all taste the same, are made to a price which is predetermined by the retailer, and the final wine lacks attitude, identity and soul. The winemaker has to deliver despite these cuts in his margin, and in so doing the final wine is compromised. It is becoming nothing more than a simple commodity.

This is not a phenomenon that is unique to wine. Smoked salmon used to be a very expensive, rare and genuinely special food. Its texture was a delight, as you chewed its juicy, intense, fine, subtle flavours, which were infused with savoury and spicy scents from the smokehouse. Nowadays most mass-market smoked salmon sold in the supermarkets is farmed in such great quantities under dubious conditions that it is no longer something rare, scarce and exceptional but instead tastes of absolutely nothing. I understand why consumers pay for such tasteless rubber, but I think it is madness. The only thing one can taste of the profuse farmed smoked salmon is the lemon juice and pepper which is sprinkled liberally on each slice to give the fish some flavour. We all perceive smoked salmon as a treat and a luxury, but in truth the farmed volume product has been so debased that it no longer represents the best in fish.

The same principle applies to meat, where again mass production, whether for chicken, lamb, pork or beef, has dramatically reduced its flavour and character. Prices have fallen, for sure (although they seem to be on the rise now), but the quality of much cheap supermarket meat is poor. The water content is high, the meat is not hung for long enough to enhance flavour and the texture is lacking when compared with the free-range organic alternatives.

There is still a delicious alternative to mass-produced farmed salmon, and it tastes distinctly different. Well-hung free-range meat from a good butcher also tastes completely unlike the alternative. If you've ever tried a flame-grilled, grass-fed, free-range cut of beef from the Argentinean Pampas, or wild Alaskan line-caught smoked salmon, you'll know what I mean.

So back to wine: the average price paid for a bottle of wine today is around £6. The tax alone on a bottle at this price accounts for more than half the total cost of the bottle. In fact, it is two taxes – excise duty and VAT. The government charges us VAT on the value of the excise duty, a tax on another tax, just to make sure we are fully taxed on our alcohol. Add the additional cost of the glass bottle, label, capsule and closure, not to mention the cost of bottling and packaging, results in rather less than £1 for the value of the liquid inside the bottle. This unimpressive wine will be mass-produced and created to meet that price point. The final wine will taste synthetic and lack definition, intensity, character and flavour. There could also be a hideous concoction of chemicals to cause all sorts of potential hazards. The simple truth is that by paying a little bit more for a bottle of wine the enhanced quality is disproportionately increased. This is because the duty on wine is a flat rate per bottle, so the proportion of the wine's price which is accounted for in tax is diminished as the price rises. This leaves more money to be spent on the quality of the liquid inside the bottle.

It reminds me of the story of the father who walks into a restaurant with his son. He gives the young boy three 10p coins to play with to keep him occupied. Suddenly the boy starts choking and going blue in the face. The father realises the boy has swallowed the coins and starts slapping him on the back. The boy coughs up two of the 10p coins, but is still choking. Looking at his son, the father is panicking, shouting for help. A well-dressed, attractive and serious-looking woman in a blue business suit is sitting at the bar reading a newspaper and sipping a cup of coffee. At the sound of the commotion, she looks up, puts her cup down, neatly folds the newspaper, places it on the counter, gets up from her seat and makes her way, unhurried, across the restaurant. Reaching the boy, the woman carefully pulls down his pants, takes hold of his testicles and starts to squeeze and twist, gently at first and then ever so firmly... tighter and tighter! After a few seconds the boy convulses violently and coughs up the remaining 10p, which the woman deftly catches in her free hand. Releasing the boy's testicles, the woman hands the coin to the father and walks back to her seat at the bar without saying a word. As soon as he is sure that his son has suffered no ill effects, the father rushes over to the woman and starts thanking her saying, *"I've never seen anybody do anything like that before – it was fantastic. Are you a doctor?"*

"No," the woman replied. *"I work for the Inland Revenue."*

There really *is* an alternative to mass-produced bland wine which doesn't have to cost the earth. I have discovered a small group of vineyard owners scattered around the world who are inspired to produce something rather special in small parcels from their bit of land and which represent exceptional value.

Compromise is for relationships, not for wine!

Hugh Johnson wrote, *"The point of drinking wine is to drink what thrills you."* There are some special wines created by passionate and determined individuals who have followed their dreams and, against the odds, have triumphed in producing the most exquisite nectar. These are stylish wines with individuality and real character produced with flair on a relatively small scale. Perhaps the reason I believe in these people is because I am completely bored with tasting shabby, miserable wine blends which have no definition, sense of place, individuality or identity. Wine is to be enjoyed heartily, but as my late mother used to say, *"Life is too short to drink poor wine."*

I think Robert Mondavi, the renowned American wine producer, was right when he said, *"Wine to me is passion. It's family and friends. It's warmth of heart and generosity of spirit. Wine is art. It's culture. It's the essence of civilisation and the art of living."*

Wine does give pleasure; sometimes just a fleeting pleasure, but sometimes the kind of pleasure which I believe is far more profound.

My job is to nose out the finest wines, often off the beaten track, scattered around the world. You and I are searching for the same thing, but what should we both be looking for in a wine? The answer is simply personal excitement and enjoyment. What we want is to pay a reasonable price for a really fabulous experience. As Jeremy Clarkson might say, I'm searching for a Ferrari in a bottle for the price of a Škoda.

It is this feeling which the supermarkets and newspaper offers play on: *"50% off,"* they scream. *"Buy one case of wine and get a second free of charge,"* the text declares. *"This case should cost £79.00, but we are discounting it down to £30.00 for a limited period."*

Everyone wants a special deal, and some of the supermarkets, larger retailers and mail-order outfits are determined to appear to offer extraordinary bargains. There is a danger, though, that at 50% off, either the original price was inflated, or the normal margins on the bottle are excessively high.

Recently I came across a supermarket offering discounted champagne during Wimbledon week. The offer was half-price champagne down from £31.00 a bottle to £15.50. It was a champagne I had never heard of, and since some of the non-vintage Grande Marque champagnes such as Veuve Clicquot, Pol Roger and Bollinger are retailed at the early thirty-pound level, there is no way in my opinion that this offer was genuine. The proper retail price for this unknown champagne should have been about £20.00 a bottle at most, so the offer was really just offering a few pounds off the authentic price of a very average-quality champagne. The perception of the deal and the reality of the offer were poles apart. It's all very well saying *caveat emptor*, but this is deceptive, contemptible, debases the wine industry and treats consumers as fools.

What I'm looking for in a wine, on the other hand, is something exciting and distinctive, a bottle you would be seduced by in your wildest dreams.

I was speaking at a dinner recently, when the man sitting next to my wife leant over to her and whispered, *"Did you ever in your wildest dreams imagine that you would marry a wine merchant?"* My wife replied, *"My husband doesn't appear in my wildest dreams!"*

So I'm searching for genuine natural flavours, not synthetic confected ones. I'm looking for the free-range equivalent, the line-caught wild option, rather than the mass-produced farmed one. I'm hunting for exceptional wines which don't have a well-known expensive brand name for which you pay a premium. Some well-known brands are very expensive in relation to the quality of the liquid inside the bottle. How much of the bottle's cost goes into advertising? Often the wines I discover are close to a well-known vineyard, or in the neighbouring village, on similar soil. If you buy the well-known Châteauneuf-du-Pape, you will pay a premium for the name, whereas if you buy the less-well-known Sablet from a neighbouring Côtes-du-Rhône Villages, it will be half the price and very close in quality to the Châteauneuf.

So this book is a distillation of the stories and amusing anecdotes garnered over twenty years of seeking out the finest wines from small, little-known boutique vineyards. It gives a glimpse of the mysterious world behind the label to reveal the crucial factors in a professional wine buyer's decision to purchase. In so doing, many of the answers to those questions you've always wanted to ask, but never dared, are disclosed.

"I can certainly see you know your wine. Most of the guests who stay here wouldn't know the difference between Bordeaux and claret."
John Cleese playing the part of Basil Fawlty in *Fawlty Towers*

OK, let's start by debunking the idea that if you don't know anything about wine, in some way your view is not valid. I don't know much about art or music, but it certainly doesn't stop me having an opinion about which pictures and which pieces of music I prefer. Wine is similar to art and music: it is *all* about personal taste. You might prefer a Picasso, but I like my daughter Ella's colourful drawings from school. I like Supertramp, whilst you might prefer Madness. I can put an argument together to support my personal choice: it is purely subjective, this is about my sensation and my experience. For example, I may be reminded of a moment or a place or a beautiful piece of art or music that I just love. Knowing little about it, I can still tell you what I enjoy viewing and listening to, because it appeals to one of my senses.

Appreciating wine is the same, although of course more senses are being excited in an intoxicating cocktail of sight, smell and taste. On my wine courses many people have questioned the descriptions you read on a wine list, telling me that they don't pick up any flavours of coconut, lanolin or sawdust. It is confusing to hear that a particular wine smells of truffles, but what on earth is that flavour if it isn't truffles to you?

So how do I go about selecting wine? The first thing to do is look at the wine's appearance – does it have "legs" when you swirl it around the glass? This indicates the level of alcohol in the wine. Do swirl it, since this helps the wine breathe and release its hidden flavours. The legs, or tears, are the streams of glycerol running down the inside of the glass. The tears are seen better when the alcohol level rises above 13 per cent.

Look at the different colours in a red wine between the rim at the edge of the glass and the core middle of the liquid. Youthful red wines tend to have a purple rim, while older wines will develop a tawny brown rim as they age. How deep and intense is the colour? The more deep and intense the better. I'm looking for wines with concentration and character; I don't want wishy-washy watery wines – I want wines with "focus".

Youthful white wines tend to have a green tinge at the rim. White wines which have been aged in oak tend to be a deeper yellow in appearance, in contrast to a more translucent unoaked wine, such as Sauvignon Blanc or Chablis.

Next I sink my nose deep into the glass. Does it smell musty, of wet sacks or wet socks? If it does, it is corked and should be rejected. This is particularly true of wines when you try them in a restaurant. To arrive

11

at their selling price, restaurants often multiply the cost of the wine by three or more and then suggest that you should pay a 10–15% service charge on top. If the wine isn't exactly right, particularly given the price, I always send it back. It could also be oxidised, due to a faulty cork, which allows air to enter the bottle through a gap between the glass and the cork. The fill level could be low, so giving a larger gap between the top of the wine and the cork – the wine will age and oxidise much more quickly as a result. It could also be the cork itself which allows air into the bottle, causing it to oxidise too quickly. This manifests itself in an oxidised sherry-like aroma, with the smell of fresh fruit no longer present.

The wine could also be faulty as a result of being stood up for a long period rather than kept on its side. The cork will dry out if the wine is not left in contact with it. Too many wines are ruined by not being kept in a dark, temperature-controlled cellar, and are often stored in the main restaurant area, where the wine warms up and cools down each day, destroying the finer, more subtle flavours in the wine.

Does it smell of any particular fruit? If it smells of blackcurrants, this may well indicate that it has Cabernet Sauvignon in the blend. If it smells of lychees, it is probably Gewürztraminer, or if it smells of gooseberries it is probably Sauvignon Blanc. There is always a danger that the wine in your glass may even smell of grapes. Is the bouquet strong or weak? Most important of all, do I like the bouquet?

Finally I taste the wine, drawing air into my mouth at the same time, swirl it around and enjoy all those different flavours. The attack is the initial impression, followed by the mid-palate mouth-feel and finally the finish. How long does the taste linger in the mouth after I've swallowed it? Is it a delicious afterburn or is it bitter or sour? Attractive persistence, long after I have swallowed, is a clear sign of pedigree, and that's what I am looking for.

Some of us prefer to taste lighter red wines, made, for example, in the Beaujolais area of France and using the Gamay grape variety. Others prefer big, rich, heavier, more powerful wines made in Australia from the Shiraz grape variety. I know which I would prefer on a warm summer's day and equally on a freezing-cold winter's evening. The circumstance of the tasting is distinctly significant in one's personal enjoyment.

What I am not interested in is a "banquet wine" – a bland wine which no one finds unpleasant but is instantly forgotten and excites nobody. The wines I seek have attitude, individuality and strong character, and, like the opinions of Margaret Thatcher or Tony Blair, you'll either be thrilled by them or they will not be for you. It's all about one's own very personal and distinctly subjective appreciation.

I remember at one of my tastings at Vintners' Hall in the City of London a client told me that wine number 41 was the best wine in the room, absolutely magnificent, one of the best he had ever tasted. Another client came up to me at the same tasting and told me that wine number 41 was off and should be taken off the table immediately.

As we get older, our palate changes and develops, which makes wine selection more complicated. As we age our sense of taste is diminished, so we need stronger and more overt flavours to get the desired sensation we crave. I find that as I get older I can certainly manage a stronger, hotter curry, which in days gone by would have had me running for a cold beer.

A wine matures in bottle, but in the opposite direction: the flavours become less simple and shrill and more complex and interesting. The primary fruit of youth gives way to the secondary and more subtle flavours of middle age, before the wine finally dies and turns to vinegar.

Whilst individual personal subjective appreciation is crucial, there are some absolutes which indicate quality – some things which mark a particular wine out as being "fine", in the same way that a piece of music by Beethoven might be considered classier than a melody composed by a Grade 1 pianist. This is a technical thing. You may not appreciate a great opera, but *La Bohème* is nevertheless a very fine work of art.

So what is the best in wine? How do you know whether the liquid in your glass is fine wine or cheap plonk, without consulting the label and considering the price?

Without marketing and promotion, and just armed with a trusty wineglass, how would you know whether the liquid in your glass is any good, irrespective of whether you like it or not? If I presented ten paintings to you, all created by gifted amateur painters, and I included one obscure masterpiece amongst them, would you be able to pick out the expensive one?

There are two things which create big differences in quality in wine. The first is yield. If you have a vineyard which is, let us say, one acre in size and you pick ten tonnes of grapes from that acre and then squash them into wine, the quality will not be as good as if you only took three tonnes of grapes from the same site, assuming of course there is no disease. This is called the yield from the vineyard, and yield can be controlled by careful pruning of the grapes during the growth cycle to ensure consistent quality. The more grapes that are produced on each vine, after a point, the lower the quality of the resultant wine. Higher yields tend to dilute the wine and produce lower concentration, lower intensity, lower complexity and less flavour in the wine. Fine, concentrated, characterful wine can only be produced from smaller yields.

So much so that in France the rules of wine production laid down by the state in the Appellation d'Origine Contrôlée legislation are designed to ensure lower yields to guarantee the quality of fine wines to protect the consumer. Yield is measured in hectolitres produced from each hectare of ground (hl/ha). Top wines will generally be below 50hl/ha and the focus of a wine dissipates dramatically after 65hl/ha.

The second important factor in determining quality is the age of the vines. In the first five years of a vine's life it does not normally make fine-quality wine. To make a good wine the roots of the vine need time to become well established. The roots need to descend deep into the soil in search of nutrients over time. It is part of the vine's natural cycle that, as it ages, so it produces fewer grapes, but of finer quality and with more personality. A vine can live for 100 years, but towards the end of its life it will produce very small quantities of exceptionally good grapes, which in turn will make fine wine. Finally it will die. (You can see the age of the vines in the vineyard by looking at the trunk of the vine. The thicker the trunk, the older the vine.)

My view is that after ten years a vine will produce decent wine, but it will improve as it gets older. 30-year-old vines are probably at their peak in terms of quality and quantity. The French sometimes even put *vieilles vignes* on their labels to indicate that the wine is better than young-vine wine to try to aid their marketing.

As the vine ages, so its roots delve deeper into the earth to find the water and nutrients it needs to survive. As the roots become more extensive, so the grapes pick up more of the trace elements in the soil, and these impart subtle, more complex flavours to the grapes, which with faithful winemaking, are then revealed in the final wine. The flavour of the wine can be an expression of what the French call *"terroir"*. Terroir has become a somewhat mystical term and is made up of a combination of soil, climate, aspect and place. For true Burgundians the Pinot Noir grape is just used as an instrument to express the local geography. The south-east facing hills in the relatively cool northern climate of Burgundy produce a wine with bright fruit flavours, higher acidity and a long, tingling, intense sensation which remains in the mouth well after you have swallowed the wine – the finish.

It is the taste in your glass which can be a pure reflection of the *terroir*, the aspect to the sun, the soil, the grape variety and the climate of that vineyard. The winemaker may well decide that there are certain natural factors in the wine which he or she prefers to conceal or enhance during the winemaking process by manipulating what nature intended. For example, in a cold marginal climate sugar can be added during the fermentation process, to be turned into alcohol by the yeast to give a naturally light, insipid wine a bit more weight and oomph. In a hot climate, the wine may have acidity added in the form of tartaric acid to reduce the heavy dumpiness in a big wine which perhaps suffers from too much alcohol. As one French winemaker commented to me, it is like putting make-up on a face. The wine appears better than its intrinsic qualities, but a great wine will not need make-up, like a beautiful girl; its greatness will shine through naturally, as characterised by a combination of concentration, intensity, balance, complexity and length.

Concentration is appreciated through both appearance and taste, showing, for instance, deeper, denser yet clear colour and more character in reds. In whites, it is the opposite of a watery, dilute, insipid wine, lacking in flavour and rather tasteless. Another description I use for concentration is focus – there's just more flavour in your glass.

Intensity is demonstrated through how pronounced the fruit flavours appear. This is revealed in the levels of fruit acidity, liveliness and zing in both red and white wines. Cooler climates tend to produce wines with greater intensity. One of the many attractions of Argentinean red wine is its refreshing fruit acidity, which is derived from the coolness of high Andean vineyards.

Balance is fundamental and the most important factor in quality wine. All the components such as fruit, acid, oak, tannin and alcohol should be moulded into a harmonious whole, all knitted neatly together with none of the qualities out of line with the others. A wine which has too much of one of these attributes – alcohol, for example – will never be a great wine. The level of alcohol may obscure the fruit character and make the wine appear "dumpy" and overweight, leaving a hot burning sensation at the back of the throat.

A wine may have too much acid and not enough fruit, which will make it appear lean, mean and bitter. It is the acidity in white wine which enables it to age. There could be too much oak flavour in the wine, which obscures the fruit – this was a problem with the earlier Chardonnays from Australia. There may also be too much tannin in a wine, often found in youthful fine red wines. This is the roughness appreciated on the inside of the mouth, similar to the sensation experienced from a strong cup of tea. As these wines mature, the tannins become less firm. The tannins are produced from the grape skin and are essential if red wine is to age.

Complexity is defined by the mixture of different attractive flavours that you detect on the nose and on the palate. During the ageing process of a red wine, it loses some of its simple fresh primary youthful fruit flavours and starts to develop other secondary, more vegetal farmyard flavours – animal, smoky, undergrowth, cigar, mocha, truffle and even leathery aromas – which, in spite of their descriptions, contribute to the complexity and quality in a well-aged, delicious wine. For white wines the complexity is driven by the aromas and blend of fruit characters balanced by toasty vanilla oak, honeyed flavours and a minerality derived from the soil, such as the limestone that is imbued in the great Burgundian whites or that flintiness in the top Sauvignons from the Loire Valley in France.

Length on the "finish" is the time the taste remains in the mouth after you have swallowed the liquid. The longer a sumptuous taste lingers on the palate, the better the wine and the more pleasurable the experience.

Can you judge a wine by its cost? The short answer is no.

If you believe in the market, price is derived from the demand and supply of scarce resources. If consumers are persuaded through skilful marketing that a particular wine or brand, made in limited quantities, is worth buying at a particular price, sales of the product at that price will rise. Consumers cannot be underestimated, and however good the marketing, buyers are shrewd and will not continue to purchase poor-quality wine. The sale of Beaujolais Nouveau in the UK is a good example. This was a brilliantly marketed product, but eventually consumers realised that it was lacking in quality and wasn't worth the ever-increasing price determined by extraordinary marketing hype. In truth, much better value wines can be found amongst the Beaujolais Crus such as Fleurie, Juliénas, Moulin-à-Vent and Morgon. The days of pretentious wine marketeers bringing out an expensive, substandard well-known branded wine from France are over. People will not drink a wine which has rough, bitter tannins and tastes like someone has just sawed through your tongue because they think they ought to. To my relief, I have found people are more refreshingly honest, better informed and less intimidated nowadays.

A quality wine which is well crafted, good value and extensively marketed should sell well, because the consumer has been well advised.

The price of a bottle is determined fundamentally by what someone is prepared to pay for it. While I was studying for the Master of Wine exam, numerous blind tastings were organised for the students and lecturers, where estimated prices were found to be wildly inaccurate after tasting a mystery wine. Here we had wine professionals at the top of their game (there are only just over 300 MWs worldwide today) who still struggled to identify the value of the wine in front of them. So how can the average *bon viveur* be expected to know what value to place on a taste? This is the enigma posed by the contents of the bottle, but if the wine has the combination of concentration, intensity, balance, complexity and length then it should be worth more than a wine that doesn't.

The situation is further confused by another element of subjectivity in wine drinking – namely the circumstances of the tasting and how you are feeling at that moment. This will also have a bearing on how the wine tastes to you. If you are in a stressful work situation in a restaurant, for example, entertaining a very important and difficult client who has an ability to cause distress, the wine, whatever it is, will not taste as good as if you are relaxed with good friends on holiday in a beautiful location in the sunshine. It has been found that if you are happy, the wine you are drinking tastes better. I have often been asked why it is that when you taste wine while on holiday in France at a *dégustation*, it tastes delicious, but bring it back to the UK and it really doesn't taste very good at all. Some suggest that wine, therefore, doesn't travel.

As an importer of Australian wine that comes by boat around the world to the UK, I can tell you this is just not true. That is as long as it travels away from the engine room and below the water-line of the boat. The reason a wine brought home from abroad doesn't taste so good is because the ambience and your palate have not travelled. When you taste a pretty acidic red wine in France during the summer, when it is hot and you are happy on holiday, the acidity is refreshing in the heat. Bring the wine back to the generally colder UK, after a stressful day at work, and the acidity is now marked, no longer refreshing, just harsh, mean and unpleasant. While in France, you may well enjoy a tannic red wine with rich food. The tannins may blend and complement the richness of the food in France, but ship the wine back to the UK and drink the wine on its own or with less rich food and the wine tastes rough and unready to drink. It is exactly the same wine, but just not sampled in the same environment, with the same food, and consequently it tastes very different.

There has always been a huge rivalry between the winemakers of France and Australia, and one French winemaker was invited over to an Australian winery to sample some of the Australian's trophy wines. As the Frenchman tasted through the bottles with the Aussie, he asked, *"Where exactly does this wine come from?"* The Australian replied, *"That wine in your glass comes from the vines right outside the window of this winery here."*

After a long pause and a Gallic shrug the Frenchman exclaimed, *"It doesn't travel very well, does it?"*

The good news is that this battle between the Old and New Worlds has improved the quality of wine across the board, and it will travel well, whether it is from France or Australia. It is not wine that doesn't travel well, it is us!

The food which accompanies the wine will also have a big impact on how the wine is appreciated. If you eat raw smoked salmon with a red wine, the wine will taste bitter and acidic, however good it is, because the tannins in the red wine fight with the salt in the raw fish.

In conclusion, the appreciation of wine is fraught with outside influences affecting the way we perceive the liquid in the glass. Even the glass itself can affect that impression. This is coupled with subjective personal views, partially influenced by advertising. But in the end, behind the label there are fundamental principles which determine whether a wine can be objectively considered fine quality.

"Life should not be a journey to the grave with the intention of arriving safely in an attractive and well-preserved body, but rather to skid in sideways – Chardonnay in one hand, chocolate in the other – body thoroughly used up, totally worn out and screaming, 'wahey, what a ride!'"
Adapted from Hunter S. Thompson

Surprisingly, I don't receive a lot of sympathy from family or friends as I set off on a wintry, cold, grey English January morning to explore some of the smaller off-the-beaten-track vineyards in sunny summery Australia. It is, of course, a hard-working journey of discovery. Some people think that wine merchants swan through life serenely, gliding effortlessly along the surface of the water: but in fact, beneath the surface, under the water, well… yes, you're right, there's bugger all going on down there either!

We are, as a breed, paddling furiously beneath that seemingly calm surface; margins are low and competition is extreme. To succeed, it is necessary to trawl around a large number of vineyards, tasting a lot of wine in the pursuit of liquid perfection, or at least something which is worth much more than its price. You must have a good palate, and it's essential to know the tastes of your customers. Once you've tasted a hundred wines almost immediately after breakfast, some of the romance of wine begins to disappear. It's also important to be a good negotiator.

My travels start on a crisp, dark early morning in January driving to Heathrow airport. I'm becoming famous, I think, and as the cab driver looks at me in his mirror, I realise he is trying to remember who I am. *"I'm the famous Wine Explorer,"* I helpfully reply to his quizzical look, to which he replies, *"I was just wondering which terminal you're leaving from?"*

18 hours later, tired, jetlagged, but a heck of a lot warmer, I drive down towards Margaret River, a three-hour journey south of Perth in Western Australia. I stop at a garage and fuel up on one of their amazingly delicious pastry pies filled with beef, spices, vegetables and Stilton cheese. The land looks brown and parched, the smell of eucalyptus hangs in the air, and as I pour my crumpled self out of the car at dusk, I can hear the orchestra of crickets tuning up for the night.

I have managed to persuade some friends to let me stay with them. Christopher Harding runs the local vine nursery. He supplies most of the Margaret River vineyards, so he knows where all the dead vines are buried. Christopher is a source of cogent advice, and he also gives me an assurance that there won't be any snakes in my bedroom – well, not on my first night. I can't bear snakes.

The following morning, refreshed and ready for almost anything, I set off for my first vineyard visit. On the way I buy a small bag of apples, which I use sporadically during the day to sharpen up my palate. The acidity in the apple energises the taste buds, making them highly sensitive to different flavours and generally more acute.

This first call is a dingy old shack, located down a muddy track off some godforsaken gravelly unsealed road. I do search for wines off the beaten track, but this is getting ridiculous. I'm not even sure if my hired car is insured on this kind of mess. As I get out of the car, once the cloud of dust has dissipated and I stop coughing, there, behind the shack, are the green leafy vines, resplendent with tiny little green berries still needing a lot more sunshine and time to bring them to ripeness. It is January and the harvest will not take place until early March in Australia. The bright-green vines provide a distinct contrast with the rest of the barren, brown landscape. Below the vines, in the distance, towards the horizon, I can see the deep-blue Indian Ocean shimmering in bright sunshine. I'm slightly scared as a large vineyard dog bounds up towards me. I could never be a postman. I like dogs, but this one would lick me to death if she could. The owner eventually arrives and calls off my new friend, who I suspect may not be the most efficient guard dog.

Most vineyards seem to have dogs. They are supposedly trained to frighten off the birds which try to steal the plump sweet ripe grapes just before the vintage is picked. The vineyard owner tells me that "Barks" is less effective than he would ideally like. One afternoon the dog was seen with what looked like blood dripping from its mouth. The winemaker was rather pleased at the thought that the dog's brutality towards birds might discourage them from stealing his grapes, only to discover that it wasn't blood after all. The dog had been quietly and discreetly checking whether the grapes were indeed fully ripe.

I arrive at another vineyard in Margaret River, which is hosting a large number of guinea fowl, strutting about pecking the ground in between the rows of vines. I am informed that they are not there to make up the numbers in an *"au vin"* stew, but instead they are useful alive, eating insect pests amongst the vines and as a consequence greatly reducing the level of spray chemicals required to protect the vineyard. It's often these chemicals which can make wines taste synthetic and unpleasant, and sometimes contribute to bad hangovers.

I tasted through the wines in this Margaret River vineyard with a running commentary on how good they were, but found them all rather unbalanced; in other words, too much acid or tannin or alcohol, without the combination of all these components integrating harmoniously together. This is what I'm looking for as a basic precondition of quality: balance.

If I like a wine and it is priced sensibly, I will ask for samples to be sent to my office in the UK. I then competitively taste all the same grape varieties together in price order on my tasting bench. The wines run from the least expensive on the left of the bench to the most expensive on the right. What I hope to find is a wine which displays all the qualities of fine wine, intensity, harmony and complexity, while standing on or towards the left-hand side of the bench. The most expensive wine is not always the best, and if I find something towards the left-hand end of the bench that is better than those further to the right, then I have discovered something of greater value than its price. There is no time for the average consumer to taste an array of wines prior to choosing his or her favourite, unless you go to an independent wine merchant's tasting, where you can try the wines before you buy them. As you would expect, I would recommend this, or you could act on a recommendation from a professional or an independent journalist, thereby ensuring you are not let down by a wine. If you take pot luck and buy a bottle off the shelf in a shop, you may well be disappointed.

Often the wines are not good enough to enter the competition on the tasting bench, so I thank the vineyard owner and proceed on to my next call. The main reason that the wines are unbalanced here is that the winemaker has decided to make wines with too much alcohol. To some extent this is as a result of climate and the location of the vines on a north-west-facing hill, which means the vines receive the heat of the sun in the afternoon and through into the evening. This, together with being positioned at a low height above sea level, contributes to the heat. The vines thus receive a lot of warmth in the summer and this Australian sun converts all that acid in the grape into sugary ripeness, which in turn is converted into alcohol during fermentation. Fermentation is the chemical reaction which takes place when the yeast on the outside of the grape skin joins the sugars in the juice inside the grape skin after the grapes have been through a crusher. As the yeast gobbles up the sugar, the by-products of this process are alcohol and carbon dioxide. So the more sugar there is in the grape, the greater the potential alcohol in the wine. Many Australian wines are now registering 14.5 and 15+ per cent alcohol, which for my taste is a little too high, and some of the wines at this level of alcohol can lack balance. There are some which are perfectly in balance even at this high level of alcohol, with an attractive richness, but these wines are not appropriate for all occasions. The alcohol can dominate the aroma and taste to the extent that the other components of the wine are subdued behind it. These components do not come together in harmony, which, as already stated, I believe is a prerequisite for quality.

As I was driving along in a slightly haphazard way (not from the alcohol: I'd been spitting the wine out, and not backwards, as the Irish like to describe it), with a map in one hand, a cup of coffee in the other and the steering wheel somewhere in between, I suddenly noticed this slinking slippery creature crossing the road ahead. Before I knew it, I had driven straight over a snake. I had half a mind to reverse back over it, just to make sure, but sped on nervously, wondering whether it could slither up the wheel arch and into the pedal area beneath my feet.

I remember the story of the man who found himself in court on a drink-driving charge. The council for the prosecution asked the defendant to relay the events of the evening in question to the court. The man responded by saying that he had been driving along, late at night, perfectly sober, when suddenly a police car had driven up behind him with its siren blaring out and its blue light flashing. Having stopped at the side of the road, he had walked back to the police car and answered a range of questions from the two police officers, who were sitting in the front seats, and a rather attractive young lady in a fur coat on the back seat. The police had then let him go. The prosecution thanked the man for his detailed recollection of the night's events, and then dampened the man's hopes of getting off by pointing out that the young girl in the fur coat was in fact a police Alsatian dog. I think he was banned from driving for years!

At my next call I learn the moving life story of the vineyard founder's passion for flying. Here I am taken on a drive around the vineyard and shown the different "blocks" of vines planted carefully, so that the warm north-facing slopes are mainly covered in red Cabernet Sauvignon and Shiraz vines, while the cooler south-facing slopes are home to the Sauvignon Blanc, Sémillon and Chardonnay grapes. The cooler areas will produce grapes with a higher acidity, which is what you want in a white wine from a warm area. On the perimeter of the estate I am shown an unlikely spot for an airstrip. Mike Edwards tells me that his father Brian sadly died recently of leukaemia. It was a long, slow illness which tragically killed him; a man who had always had boundless energy and an immense passion for flying. As a war widow (Brian's father had been killed flying a Lancaster bomber over Germany in 1943), Brian's mother had been given funds from a war-widow charity to help bring him up. Having benefited from this financial help as a child, Brian had decided to fly a 1943 Tiger Moth from England to Australia, along the route the great Australian aviation pioneers took, to honour the memory of his father and to raise funds for Legacy, the same charity which had supported his mother. It was a way of repaying them for their kindness and generosity during his childhood. He took off on 2nd March 1990 from RAF Binbrook in Lincolnshire, the same airfield from which his father had taken off in his Lancaster on his final bombing raid on the night of July 3rd 1943. Brian could see the south coast of England coming towards him when the crankshaft snapped and he crashed into a field in Kent. Undeterred, he started again a few weeks later, after the plane had been repaired. This time he managed the whole journey to Australia and arrived in Langley Park, Perth, on 13th May 1990. He raised an enormous sum of money in the process.

Today, the Tiger Moth Brian flew stands in all its glory in the Edwards Vineyard as a memorial to a great man who seized his dream and took a small plane across the world to raise money for something worthwhile.

The wines all have a similar house style at Edwards Vineyard, displaying a softness and a smoothness, a charm which makes them approachable early, in both the reds and the whites.

The Edwards Vineyard, being close to the sea, captures the breeze to keep the grapes cool and to prevent the white wines from becoming "dumpy" and hot. The Edwards ferment their wine in French oak barrels, a quarter of which are brand new, and this creates a similar tone to a stylish white Burgundy. In fact, the Chardonnay I discovered is so good that it is served in the first-class cabin of Qantas Airways.

The following morning my journey continued from Margaret River up to Perth and then a short flight to Adelaide. This is the gateway to the renowned vineyard areas of Barossa and McLaren Vale. I stayed in the little picturesque town of Glenelg, which is on the beach and a superb place to set up camp if you can dodge the trams.

My favourite vineyard in McLaren Vale is the small Brini Estate Vineyard. The Brini family has been growing grapes in this part of Australia since 1953 and McLaren Vale is now widely recognised as being the finest area in Australia for producing Shiraz. John Brini runs the family estate and the wines are staggeringly good. If, like me, you like big, powerful, fruity wines, these are outstanding. I tasted through the collection of their wines, which all had a depth and concentration which I am always searching for in a quality red wine. It is the age of the vines which contributes to the greatness of this little-known vineyard. The Shiraz vines were originally planted in 1947. The flagship

Sebastian Shiraz is named after John's father, who was tragically killed in a tractor accident in the vineyard.

I'm searching for a Shiraz red wine which is going to give the most famous and expensive wine in Australia some competition, a bit of a run for its money. I'm looking for something to go up against the well-known Penfolds Grange, for which you can pay thousands of pounds a case. This Brini Shiraz has something of the style, concentration and power of that famous Australian wine, but is a fraction of the cost. I have discovered my Ferrari in a bottle for the price of a Škoda.

I thought the Brini Shiraz was excellent and shipped some of the wine to the UK. Some months later a delighted John Brini rang me in the UK at some ungodly hour to tell me that his Sebastian Shiraz had just been selected for the Qantas first-class cabin. Another one!

While I am in Glenelg, the papers are full of the tragic mauling of a young teenager who had gone swimming near Brisbane at dusk. A four-metre bull shark attacked her, and she sadly died in hospital of blood loss. I wasn't too worried about sharks in Adelaide, as Brisbane is miles away, until I read in the following day's local newspaper that a seven-metre great white shark had just been seen two kilometres off Glenelg beach itself, where I was staying. I decided on balance not to go swimming in the sea; I'd rather deal with the salesman in the vineyards!

I'm late for my next call, so I step on it, and as I accelerate around a corner I come face to face with a large brown lump sitting in the middle of the road. I brake and swerve around a big dead kangaroo. As you drive along the roads in Australia it seems you are never far from a yellow sign with a black kangaroo painted on it. At night kangaroos are a real pest and a danger to drivers. They don't have clear night vision and are often hit on the road, causing a lot of accidents and damage.

I travel from Glenelg to the Barossa Valley. Away from the coast it is warmer and the climate is ideal, so it is not surprising that the history of wine this area dates back for well over a hundred years. Initially I am not impressed with the huge, blockbuster, alcoholic, dense red wines I taste, until I stumble across Turkey Flat Vineyards. Here the elegance and slightly lower alcohol mitigates towards the most stylish wines made from their 100-year-old vines. These are beautifully balanced, simply delicious wines.

Next, down to Tasmania, where it is significantly cooler than on the Australian mainland, and so Rieslings and Pinot Noirs can compete. Hobart is a striking city where the wombat and wallaby are replaced by the Tasmanian devil. As you would expect, the fish is stupendous, and I would recommend Fish Frenzy at Elizabeth Street Pier for the best and most reasonably priced fish restaurant. Driving east out of Hobart I discovered the little village of Cambridge, and a few miles further north I came across Darren and Jackie Brown who run Puddleduck Vineyard. I was struck by the warmth of their welcome and the fun they were both having, together with their young family, dogs and copious, yes you guessed it, ducks. Tasmania is renowned for its world-class sparkling wines, but Riesling, Sauvignon Blanc, Chardonnay, Pinot Gris and Pinot Noir all have a bright future here, served as they are by the cooler maritime climate. The fizz from this vineyard was aptly named Bubbleduck, and the curious red sparkling Merlot was even more aptly branded as Muddleduck. This is apparently delicious with... er, turkey and cranberry sauce, and I can imagine it would be.

My favourite vineyard in Tasmania was the Craigow Vineyard, run by Barry and Cathy Edwards. Barry is a surgeon, and when I tasted his wines I was immensely impressed with all of them. The only problem was the price, which sadly was too much for me to be able to sell the wine successfully in the UK.

Flying on to the Yarra Valley, just east of Melbourne, I discover a delightful old man, born in 1925, who has an inexhaustible passion for winemaking. He is self-taught, and it is in this vineyard that I find what I have really been looking for. It is here that I find an absolutely amazing red wine which has been nurtured and brought to life with consummate skill by a dedicated and passionate man who really understands wine. This is a masterpiece. It is an opulent, seductive, concentrated red wine which is beautifully harmonious and an utter joy. Made in the same way as a Grand Cru from France, from older vines producing startling quality, this wine is produced in tiny quantities, is simply delicious and, more importantly, reasonably priced. Ian makes 1,200 cases in total across his range each year, and only 100 cases of this particular wine, but wow it is good. It is the holy grail – it is what I have been searching for, and it is a fabulous find. This is what makes it all worthwhile. This wine really is a Bentley in a bottle. As I taste it, I try not to look too excited. Much later, I entered this wine in the 2009 Quality Drink Awards and was delighted to receive the winning trophy for the category of red wines over a tenner.

Ian laments the scourge of foxes in the Yarra Valley. Thank goodness hunting is allowed here in Australia, he says, rather pointedly. The vineyard manager covers the rows of vines with huge white nets as the harvest approaches and the birds get more interested in eating the ripe grapes. The nets keep the birds away, or, if foolhardy enough to try and penetrate the nets, the birds will get caught and die inside them. Certainly not of hunger. Ian told me the story of a wily fox he discovered one evening at twilight walking down a row of vines in his vineyard. The fox stops and burrows under the netting to get inside, where he devours the already caught dead birds, and then he is glimpsed standing on his hind legs, leaning against the trellis wire, devouring the grapes for his pudding. Mr Fox then burrows out of the netting and saunters home replete. It reminds me of the wine snob who, when he was offered grapes for his pudding replied, *"I am not in the habit of taking my wine in the form of pills."*

Ian also told me the story of a bull which lived in the field just beyond the vineyard. On one occasion, having finished the fermentation, he chucked out all the old pips and skins left over in the bottom of the vat into the field. A couple of hours later he discovered the bull staggering about the field, and then watched as the animal sat down rather haphazardly, cross-eyed and cross-legged, on a bench in the field, awaiting an enormous hangover.

The Yarra Valley is one of the cooler climates of Australia, close to the sea on the east coast, so the vines take a little longer to ripen and consequently display an enhanced depth. It was here that the famous champagne house of Moët & Chandon first made fizz in Australia. Champagne grapes need a cool climate to preserve the acidity which is so important in the wine. But not only that: it is a climate that works particularly well for Pinot Noir, the most important grape variety in the champagne blend. This sensitive, thin-skinned grape variety is fastidious and goes on strike when the weather is either too hot or too cold. There is a poignant moment in the film *Sideways* when Pinot Noir is described, *"Pinot needs constant care and attention… It can only grow in really specific, little tucked-away corners of the world. Only the most patient and nurturing of growers can do it… Only somebody who really takes the time to understand Pinot's potential can then coax it into its fullest expression."* (*Sideways*, 2004)

Here, in the picturesque Yarra Valley, I discover the Wedgetail Estate and the best Pinot Noir and Chardonnay I have tasted in Australia. This vineyard has only six hectares under vine, and this limited production is made even more precious by controlling the yield of each individual vine. The results are exceptional grapes with intense flavours and complexity.

My flight back to the UK is a long one, and now the hard work starts with further tasting, selection and negotiation before the final purchases are made. It will take 50 days to ship the wine from Australia to London.

As I snooze on the plane and recollect some of my experiences in Australia, my mind drifts to memories of meeting a very special lady. It was soon after meeting this beautiful girl that she dropped the bombshell that she didn't drink red wine. I laughed uproariously and then a little nervously and then with wide-eyed amazement gulped for air and whispered, *"You're joking, right, that's just a funny line to wind me up, huh?"*

It was then that the sad fact dawned on me that I had fallen in love with this gorgeous girl with whom I could not share my love of wine. I also concluded that compromise is for other things apart from this delectable nectar. After a sleepless night, bottling up serious anxieties, I awoke with a plan. Somehow I had to change this woman.

Sharing a bottle is one of the most enjoyable things in life, and now I could see years ahead of being denied the opportunity to enjoy a bottle of red wine with the woman I loved. Hangovers or abstinence were the only options unless I could change her taste buds.

I started her off on rosé, which, after a dubious start, she started to knock back and quite enjoy. Next came Beaujolais – yes, this was quite difficult for both of us, because *"life is too short to drink Beaujolais"*. Well, it certainly was for her, and it definitely is for me. How I laboured in an uphill struggle drinking that light fruity nonsense which should really only be drunk in the summer, preferably chilled so much that you can hardly taste it. It has to be VERY hot to drink that glorified Ribena. It's not surprising that Beaujolais Nouveau sank without trace. After yet another bottle I tremulously enquired, *"What do you think of Beaujolais?"* She smiled sympathetically or ironically: *"Yes it's not bad – quite sweet really."* I tried not to let my face give away my amazement and TOTAL disagreement.

I toiled and toiled and finally took her on to Pinot Noir – a rather more distinguished lighter red wine whose nobility shines through. It's not surprising that some Duke of Burgundy many years ago had all the Beaujolais vines uprooted and threatened the guillotine to anyone who planted the Beaujolais grapevine Gamay rather than Pinot Noir on this hallowed French turf.

Finally, one night while my girlfriend was deeply ensconced in a crossword puzzle, I quietly, even stealthily, passed her a glass of Aussie Shiraz – one of the biggest, most powerful, alcoholic red wines in the world, and retreated swiftly out of the room to avoid the flak. *"Hmm, this is nice, what's this?"* She smiled as my nose came around the door. *"Will you marry me?"* I asked.

"Yes, as long as you promise never to give me cheap Beaujolais again!"

My wife Nicola now prefers red to white, and occasionally needs my help to finish the bottle.

"The point of drinking wine is… to taste sunlight trapped in a bottle, and remember some stony slope in Tuscany or a village by the Gironde."
John Mortimer

Wine is created after the grapes are harvested in the vineyard and squashed in the winery.

Reading between the vines, the big question is: when do you pick the grapes? In the Northern Hemisphere it is normally at the end of September or early October, although in the warm summers we have been experiencing recently the harvest has begun as early as August in Southern Europe. The level of alcohol is increasing in wine worldwide because of global warming and climate change. A spate of hotter summers has ripened the grapes more fully and more quickly, producing less acid and more sugar in the ripe grapes, which is converted during fermentation into higher levels of alcohol. Too much alcohol may obscure the fruit character of the wine. This, in my view, also prevents a wine from ageing gracefully, and may shorten the life of a fine wine. The 2003 vintage in Bordeaux, produced in a summer which was very hot, has higher levels of alcohol than the norm, and it will be interesting to see how these wines develop over the next few decades.

English wine is benefiting from this increase in global temperatures. There are now over 400 vineyards in the UK, and our wines are winning international awards – particularly our fizz. My favourite is the Furleigh Estate in Dorset, which produces a delicious Classic Cuvée. There were only about 40 vineyards registered in the Domesday Book in 1086, but by the 17th century there were no vineyards in the UK at all, because the weather had cooled to such an extent that it was impossible to ripen grapes. If climate change is cyclical, I wonder whether history may repeat itself?

The grapes used for making sweet wines are picked later in October and November, once the "noble rot" has encouraged the grapes to shrivel into concentrated raisins. It is a difficult decision to know when to pick, particularly in marginal climates, where bad weather can follow in the autumn. Pick now while the grapes are slightly unripe, dry and healthy, or wait until after the rain has stopped and the grapes have had time to ripen more fully. The problem with waiting is that the weather may not improve. With insufficient wind to dry off the grapes, this can either cause mildew or cause the grapes to split from the sudden addition of fresh rainwater gulped up from the roots: and then rot sets in through the cracked grape skins.

Rain will certainly increase the volume of the vintage and can therefore increase the potential revenue from the vineyard, as long as the wine doesn't suffer from dilution and quality is not compromised.

Grape picking should take place at optimum ripeness. Potential alcohol and the amount of sugar in the grape can be measured by using a refractometer. The sugar is the potential alcohol, since the yeasts on the grape skin will eat the sugar and produce alcohol and carbon dioxide during the fermentation process. The more sugar, the more alcohol for the yeasts to produce. In my experience, though, an experienced winemaker will taste the grapes to decide when to pick, rather than use a machine.

As I was walking high up in a Stellenbosch vineyard in South Africa, overlooking Cape Town in the distance, I remember discussing with a high-calibre winemaker from Mooiplaas vineyard called Louis Roos how he came to his decision as to when to begin the harvest. He recounted his own story of how he had been walking in the vineyard with his dog over a few days as vintage approached, tasting the grapes, each day for ripeness. On the final day, he tasted one of the grapes and as usual spat it out onto the ground. This time, and for the first time, the dog went and ate the remains of the grape which he had just spat out. The grapes were perfectly ripe – it really was time for the harvest. He organised the start of grape picking the following day.

In the more marginal climates of the Northern Hemisphere the weather tends to get worse in October; the equinoctial gales are a hazard which the New World doesn't need to worry about or deal with. This means that New World wines are generally much more consistent, with less vintage variation.

You can either pick the grapes by hand or by machine. The machine is much quicker and can work through the night when the temperature is cooler, and thus the grapes don't oxidise as much as during the day.

The machine will shake the vine vigorously and the grapes drop down onto a conveyor belt of baskets which then deposit the grapes into a truck. The problem with machine harvesting is that not only grapes drop off but everything which happens to be living on the vine drops off too (commonly known as MOG: "matter other than grapes"). This includes snails, spiders, worms and dead leaves which then need to be taken out before going into the crusher. As long as there is a sorting conveyor belt with plenty of people taking out the MOG, this should not be a problem. Hand-picking is more gentle and can be highly selective, leaving bad grapes and MOG on the vine and just picking the ripe healthy grapes. Some wines have to be hand-picked, such as Sauternes, where the individual berries covered in "noble rot" are selected carefully by hand during repeated runs through the vineyard. (The rot is a fungus which takes over the grape as it shrivels.) Picking machines just cannot make that special selection.

My first memory of harvesting grapes was in 1983 when, aged 19, I managed to get myself recruited to pick the grapes at Château Angludet in Margaux, just north of Bordeaux on the left bank of the Gironde river. An eclectic mixture of nationalities descended on the château for the six-week ordeal. There were people from Spain, France, Britain, Portugal and North Africa. Some of these individuals were running away from things – employment, wives, husbands and even the reality of life itself. Others were professional pickers moving from vineyard to vineyard. The experience does now seem like a dream, although at the time there were moments of great entertainment and joy, coupled with times which were really very hard to endure.

The harvest is an amazing, extraordinary experience. Intense, back-breaking work, starting at 8 a.m. as the sound of tractor horns arouse you from a deep alcohol-fuelled slumber. No time for breakfast, just scramble to find a few clothes, then you rush to clamber on board the trailer behind the tractor, amidst the other pickers, armed only with a pair of secateurs and a basket. The tractor takes you to the part of the vineyard that has been selected for picking on that day. The white grapes are generally picked a few weeks before the red grapes, since Sémillon and Sauvignon Blanc in Bordeaux will ripen before the Cabernet Sauvignon and Merlot. The Merlot grape variety ripens about three weeks before the Cabernet Sauvignon, and generally each of the grape varieties are planted together in the warmer or cooler sites in the vineyard.

Each of the pickers is assigned a particular row, and off you go with your little wooden basket and snip, snip, snip, as you cut bunches off from each vine, whilst saving a few juicy berries for your late breakfast. At the end of the rows is a flask of wine and a jug of water, so once you have finished your row you wait for the others to finish while you enjoy the advantage of picking quickly. Or in my case, you don't, because you seem to be doing it a lot more thoroughly and slowly than the others. Since you finish the row last, you don't get a break, and are officiously ushered on to the next row.

If you are lucky and early onto the tractors you claim a hod. This is a container that you strap to your back over your shoulders, which is filled by the pickers with grapes from their wooden or plastic pannier baskets. This is much better work, because you just stand around waiting for everyone to fill their baskets and then just walk up and accept their grapes. The hod, once filled to the brim, is emptied into the trailer by putting your head down into the truck upside down to offload the grapes from the hod on your back. The trick here is to avoid falling in yourself as you lean precariously over the truck. The joke that two of the girls liked to repeat over and over as you went to collect their grapes was, *"Have you got a hod on, Graham?"* Ho! Ho!

Having started at 8 a.m., you stop for lunch at 12 noon. While I was picking at Château Angludet, I experienced and observed a curious French lunchtime habit. After finishing the first course of soup, wine was poured into the dirty soup bowl and used to swirl around and clean the bowl, before finally drinking the wine mixed with the soup bits directly from the bowl itself! The main course was then eaten from the same wine-cleaned soup bowl. It's something I am currently trying to teach my children *not* to do.

At 1 p.m. the tractors would sound their horns again; we were taken to another spot in the vineyard, assigned a row to pick and off we would go again, cutting off the bunches of grapes, while tasting a few just to finish off pudding. The large flasks of wine, strategically positioned at the end of the rows, were getting emptier now, and once you finished your row, the keg was available to quench your thirst in the heat of the early October afternoon sunshine. We would finally be taken back to the château at 5 p.m. and a bonfire party would go on late into the night, while stories were exchanged, amongst much growing hilarity and merriment, a glass always at hand. The château would provide copious quantities of *vino* and the party would continue into the small hours. Each night and every night... It was hardly surprising that some of us never made it to breakfast during the entire six-week ordeal.

There were many entertaining incidents and extraordinary people who came to pick. There was one character who I shall never forget. His name was John Giddings and he had given up his job as an accountant and had decided to take some time out. He never stopped talking and would bring entertainment and humour to proceedings. He always drank far too much and always laughed and grinned his way through each long day, constantly telling stories and keeping us all amused. He was clever, too, completing the *Times* cryptic crossword in about ten minutes. I remember him trying to teach us all how to solve it, and in the process came up with what I believe is the best crossword clue of all time. Abcdefg.........pqrst.

The answer was five letters long... Water. Just brilliant.

As Byron wrote, *"Wine cheers the sad, revives the old, inspires the young, makes weariness forget his toil and fears her danger, opens a new world when this, the present, palls."* But he probably never picked grapes for six weeks!

I remember one evening driving a group of us to the local bar, close to the vineyard in the village of Cantenac. We consumed a few *formidable* beers, as they are called there, presented in an enormous glass. At the end of the evening, we smuggled out a glassful of brandy to enjoy when we arrived back at our mixed Château outhouse dormitory. John Giddings was given the job of holding on to this glass and not letting any of the brandy spill out during the journey back to Angludet. I drove very slowly and carefully through the fog on the way back to the Château. John was in the front seat, and held the glass nervously in both hands, out in front of him. Eventually we arrived home, excited about the long night of conversation ahead with our loving cup to pass round from hand to hand. As John opened the door, he fell out onto the grass and the brandy went with him. Urgently he picked up the glass, which wasn't broken but was distinctly empty, and sniffed. We had to all content ourselves with passing round and just nosing this empty glass, but I can still remember the gorgeous scent of the esters to this day.

The climate in the vineyard plays an important role in creating the character of a wine. In the cool climates of England, Germany and northern France the summers tend to be cooler than further south. This means that the acidity in the grapes remains more prominent, and like any fruit, more acidity means less ripeness and less sugar. Apples in England tend to be crisper and more refreshingly acidic than apples in Spain, which tend to be riper, sweeter and less crisp. That is simply because it is hotter in Spain, so more of the acidity is ripened in the sunshine into sweetness and sugar. The same applies to grapes. With lower levels of sugar, in a cooler climate, there will naturally be lower alcohol in the final wines since there is less sugar for the yeast to convert into alcohol. This explains the 8–9% alcohol levels in some German wines.

The difficulty in these climates is actually managing to ripen the grapes fully at all. In the Mosel valley in Germany the steep vineyards on either side of the river give the vines, and more importantly the grapes, an aspect which maximises their exposure to the sun. Picking these grapes is much more difficult as ropes are used to hold on to as the grape-pickers gradually descend towards the valley floor. (Over the years there have been a number of deaths as a result of accidentally letting go of the rope and suddenly falling to the bottom.) Some of the Riesling wines produced in the Mosel valley are outstanding and well worth all the endeavour and sacrifice which goes into their production.

45

For me Riesling is perhaps the most underrated white wine and should be considered the king of all the white grapes. The tension in the wine, or the fruit intensity, coupled with the fresh, crisp, lively, vivacious acidity is tingling and deliciously cutting, like a razor-sharp knife through any rich food or creamy sauce. It is the cool climate which delivers this style of lighter, brighter white wine.

The hotter climates of the Southern Hemisphere in places such as Australia and South Africa create the opposite problem. When the summers are very hot, the grapes ripen early and more completely, so more of the acidity is converted into sugar by the sunshine, and therefore there is more natural sugar in the grape to be converted by the yeasts into alcohol.

The vine's canopy (meaning the branches of the vine) can, to some degree, be manipulated in the vineyard, through trellising, so that the leaves give some protection to the grapes from direct sunlight. In a cool climate, the leaves can be removed to allow the grapes to benefit from more sunshine.

The individual grape variety itself accounts for about seventy per cent of the final character of a wine. Each variety has its own intrinsic bouquet and taste. Gewürztraminer, for example, whether from Alsace in France, Tasmania in Australia or Gisborne in New Zealand, smells – no, reeks – pungently of lychees. Sauvignon Blanc, whether from Marlborough in New Zealand, Margaret River in Australia or from the Loire Valley in France, smells of gooseberries or freshly cut grass. If you were brought up with a Siamese cat, as I was, you'll recognise and recollect an indisputably authentic, but rather differently described smell! But then again, I'm in the business of selling this wine...

Chardonnay has been described as having a melon flavour, and Chenin Blanc a citrus character. Riesling begins with a striking lime flavour, and then develops a lively bouquet of what can only be described as petrol as it gets older. Viognier has an extraordinary rich flavour of apricots, white peaches and spice.

While I was exploring the vineyards of the Ockanagan in British Columbia in Canada, I heard a true story which puts a new gloss on the ABC view of wine – Anything But Chardonnay.

In the Ockanagan, you occasionally may come across wild bears. While walking in the woods holidaymakers are encouraged to either take pepper spray with them or wear bells on their legs to warn bears of their imminent arrival, as these creatures tend to keep themselves to themselves. This is unless the mother bear has young cubs with her, in which case she can, like so many animals, be very dangerous, attacking anything, including humans, to protect her young.

One day in late summer just before vintage in British Columbia, a bear and her two cubs were spotted walking down a row of vines, having broken into the vineyard through a wire fence which they had simply sat on to get through. The three bears were observed trotting straight past the Chardonnay vineyard and on into the Syrah vineyard, where they decided to sit down in the shade of the leaves and settle in for a serious feast. No one dared to interrupt them, but everyone enjoyed the conspicuously discerning taste of the mother, who became known as the Syrah bear and was just another one of the ABC club.

Cabernet Sauvignon tends to taste of blackcurrants. Pinot Noir is cherries, Merlot is plums, Syrah is peppers and spice in a cooler climate, while Shiraz, in a hotter climate, is raspberries and rich dark fruits. Nebbiolo is tar and roses and Gamay is bubble gum.

The thickness of the red grape skin, relative to the quantity of juice inside the grape, provides both the potential tannin and colour for the final wine. For example, the Cabernet Sauvignon is a small grape with a thick skin. The wine produced from this grape variety is thus deeply coloured and tannic, which gives the wine its ability to age, by providing structure. The grape often coupled with Cabernet Sauvignon is Merlot.

The two grape varieties come together in Bordeaux in France, to produce some of the finest wines in the world. I spent most of my time at Château Angludet picking these two grapes. The Merlot is a large grape with a thin skin. The wine produced from Merlot possesses fleshy, riper, smoother flavours with higher alcohol levels, which complement the more austere tannins of Cabernet Sauvignon. The fact that the two grape varieties ripen at different times provides an insurance policy for the Bordelais, since it is unlikely that bad equinoctial weather at harvest time is going to hit both grape varieties and destroy the entire crop. There have certainly been vintages when one of the grape varieties has been wiped out completely by bad weather, such as in 1984. The blend of the two grape varieties produces a more complete character.

The Pinot Noir grape, on the other hand, is thin-skinned and very sensitive to disease, and doesn't like to be too hot or too cold. The wines produced from Pinot Noir can be the most sensual of all. In its youth the Pinot Noir produces wines tasting of raspberries, cherries, strawberries and violets, while ageing through more spicy and gamey scents as it matures in bottle.

Zinfandel is more meaty and peppery and excels in the Napa Valley, particularly at Frog's Leap, as discussed earlier. Some people believe this grape is genetically identical to the Primitivo grape from Italy, but it tastes very different in North America.

Another important factor in the vineyard which determines the character of a wine is the soil. The most important thing about soil is its ability to drain. Vines hate wet feet. Some soils impose a particular flavour on the wine. The granite of the Beaujolais hills in France can almost be tasted in the Crus and the gravel in the Graves region of Bordeaux is legendary.

The substance of the soil is also important, since very fertile soils tend to make the vine produce a huge crop and the quality of the grapes produced can be compromised as a result.

An oversimplified but nevertheless generally held view is that, to make really good wine, the vine has to struggle a little, with a poor-quality soil, possessing little fertility or nutrition. This encourages the vine to send down its roots deep into the earth to seek out the nutrition and water it needs to survive. As it strains to produce a small crop of grapes, the quality and concentration of the few grapes produced is very high. The resultant wine is likely to demonstrate more individuality, quality and character. It is in the end up to the balance of nature, which means enough sunshine to ripen the grapes and not so much rain as to dilute the final wine. There needs to be a balance in the vine between shoot growth and berry growth, which is sometimes manipulated by the vineyard manager to concentrate the energy of the vine towards optimising the quality of grapes rather than producing large quantities of foliage. This will also improve the quality of the grapes.

Too much suffering through lack of water and too much heat and the vine will die. A little hardship, on the other hand, is a good thing in providing high-quality fruit. The French call it *"la lutte raisonnée"* (the reasoned struggle), which is the way I like to bring up my children. This will strengthen the character, motivate the vine to work harder and send its roots down deeper into the soil to provide the grapes with better, more complex flavours.

Alternatively, indulgence and spoiling, where life is made too easy for the vines – perhaps by using too much fertilizer or water on the soil, or the soil just being very fertile – negates the need for the vine to work hard to produce the grapes, and the result will be a huge crop of mediocre grapes of limited quality. The vine becomes apathetic and lazy.

The amount of grape juice produced from a specific area of the vineyard is, as discussed earlier, called the yield. The more grapes that are produced on each vine, after a point, the lower quality the resultant wine will become. Higher yields tend to produce lower concentration, lower intensity, lower complexity and less flavour in wine. Fine, concentrated, characterful wine can only be produced from small yields. The French believe that you cannot really make great wine above a yield of 50 hectolitres (hl) per hectare (ha). The average yield of vines in France is 52 hl/ha. The lowest average yield for any country in the world is in Spain, where it is measured as 30hl/ha. The highest average yield for any country is 103hl/ha in Germany. This is partly because Germany produces much more white wine than red, which is less sensitive to high yields. In France the bureaucratic system to guarantee quality for the consumer is the Appellation d'Origine Contrôlée system (AOC). Originally established in France in 1905, it has been updated regularly, but yields are an important determinant of quality in individual areas. In Beaujolais red wines are permitted yields of up to 65hl/ha, whereas in Bordeaux the maximum permitted yield for red wine is 55 hl/ha for red and 65hl/ha for white. Sauternes is generally as low as 20hl/ha, where the grapes have shrivelled and lost much of their water content for this concentrated, sweet wine.

For red wines a yield of anything below 45 hl/ha is likely, in the absence of disease, to produce something special. One of the greatest red wines in the world is Château Margaux in the Médoc in Bordeaux. This is one of the Premiers Crus Classés, or first-growth wines, classified in the register in 1855. Each year the Château only produces about 12,500 cases of this top wine from 82 hectares of land. The yields are kept low to ensure high quality, and, for example, were held at 39hl/ha for the 2010 vintage of the first wine, considered one of the greatest vintages of all time.

To make great wine, you must have the balance correct in the vineyard. Even then, with fine healthy grapes brought into the winery, the winemaker has a huge challenge to translate that potential into a first-rate final wine. It is the weather, which each year may be so different in the marginal climates of Northern Europe, which gives the resultant wines their individuality, their thumbprint. One of the joys of wine is comparing the different vintages and watching how each wine develops in bottle over the years, as the bottles gradually mature over time. As Peter Finlayson, winemaker at Bouchard Finlayson in South Africa, wrote:

"Each new wine is like a new child, displaying uniqueness, offering promise, evoking a range of emotions without any guarantees. I get to be involved in

the initial development, giving my all, but once bottled and released into the world, I have to stand back and let go, quietly watching it develop and make its mark or accept criticism in the face of its exposure."

"It doesn't matter if the bottle is half full or half empty. The most important thing is there is still room for more wine."
Anon.

In New Zealand, I feel a lot safer than Australia, surrounded by sheep rather than snakes and sharks. There are 10 million sheep in New Zealand, and 5 million of them think they're humans. Some New Zealanders consider themselves to possess a sophistication which the Aussies may lack in certain circles. New Zealand wine, so their winemakers tell me, has a distinctive elegance to it. One winemaker described the difference to me in his wines when compared with Australian wines: *"Would you prefer to drink a supermodel or a Page 3 model?"*

I think the general impression one gets while drinking New Zealand wines is of their higher price and increasingly high alcohol. The fruit is powerful and intense in the whites, to the extent that you can spot the individuality and distinctiveness of a New Zealand Sauvignon Blanc compared to one from anywhere else in the world just by sinking your nose into the glass. The wine doesn't quite shout at you, but it certainly talks to you in the same way that my wife sometimes speaks to me!

Many sheep and cattle farms have been replaced by vineyards. Stainless steel equipment used in milk production and the process of pasteurisation has been quickly and effectively modified to become top-quality winemaking equipment. Even the cows seem happier.

While exploring the wines at one vineyard, I am told the amazing story of an Australian fellow called Larry, who had bought a return ticket home but fell in love with the Martinborough area and tore up his ticket and stayed. He subsequently planted a vineyard called Escarpment, which is now one of the most successful in the region.

So many small-vineyard owners do something else to begin with and then decide to get out of the rat race, follow their dream, set up a vineyard and produce their own wine. One winemaker told me it was a primeval urge to set down roots and grow something. It is a journey so often filled with great intentions, but sadly sometimes finishing with heartache, as this business is a very hard struggle. Making the wine is the easy bit – the big challenge is selling it, year in and year out. In the harsh real world, the complexity and competitiveness of the wine trade are totally unforgiving.

I take a small old-fashioned leather-seated plane down to Queenstown on South Island. As the sun rises it creates shadows on the snow-capped mountains, with the majestic Mount Cook standing tallest, overlooking beautiful turquoise lakes along the route. Central Otago is the southernmost vineyard area of New Zealand. The vines were planted as recently as the late 1980s. It is simply stunning and reminds me a little of the west coast of Scotland. The conventional wisdom had been that it was too far south to grow vines, too cold, and there would be late frost problems in the spring, which damage the flowering, and early frost damage in the autumn around harvest. In any case, the grapes wouldn't ripen properly because of a lack of sufficient warmth and sunshine. Wine is, after all, simply bottled sunshine.

One vineyard owner told me the story of his own father, who fell in love with the region and decided to plant a vineyard there. He was told he would not be purchasing his vines from the New Zealand Grape Development Corporation, the body which sanctioned new plantings. This august body took the view that the grapes wouldn't ripen this far south of the equator.

The man discovered that there was a lady further north, near Christchurch, who had decided to give up with her vineyard and was uprooting all her plants. He drove up and picked up all her vines and drove straight back down to plant his own new vineyard. He started to make wine a few years later, which then, to the surprise of the doubters, started to win awards. It was only a few years ago that international judges in a blind wine-tasting competition chose a Pinot Noir produced in this area as the very best in the world. It was this brilliant pioneering attitude that helped establish New Zealand wine.

The age of a vine, as I've written already, is important in determining quality in the final wine produced. Young vines do not, it is said, produce decent wine. As the vine ages, so the quality tends to improve and the quantity produced fall. After about seven years the vines will start to produce a good crop of reasonable-quality grapes. Until then the vines tend to produce lighter wines, lacking depth and with an unattractive "greenness" to them. However, I have discovered that there is an exception to this rule of thumb. Sometimes Pinot Noir vines in their first year will produce a small quantity of virginal grapes which when crushed can produce the most stunning gold-medal-winning wine. In the following few years the wine can be rather ordinary and revert to type, until the vines come of age.

Sadly, at my next call the vines are too young. The whites are watery, dilute and lacking either concentration or definition, while the reds are pale, simple fruity wines displaying a chemical, slightly synthetic confected fruit quality. In a few years, once the vines have aged, the wines may well improve and become more clearly defined. Central Otago has had a huge increase in vine plantings over the past ten years, and it will just take time before the wines produced are of a world-class quality. There has been an explosion of new vineyards in Alexandra, Cromwell and along the road out of Queenstown heading for Wanaka, the town beside the beautiful lake of the same name. It is here that I discover a vineyard called Rippon Valley, high up on the shore of Lake Wanaka just outside the town. The vine rows slope down towards the water with the mountains in the distance; it is probably the most beautiful vineyard site in the world.

The potential in this marginal climate is huge. A marginal climate means there is only just enough warmth and sunshine to ripen the grapes fully. Each year is a precarious risk, sometimes great, sometimes awful. It is a slow, gradual ripening process each year, which gives the final wines more character and flavour. It is a distinct improvement on a hotter climate, where the heat of the sun ripens the grapes quickly in summer over a relatively short period, but this doesn't give the vines enough time to produce grapes with higher levels of flavour. The problem with marginal climates is that there is a much greater variation in the style and quality of the final wines produced because of the fickle nature of the weather. Sometimes the wines produced in a particular vintage can be terrible as a result of wet and/or cold weather at the wrong time of year. Equally, if the weather is fine throughout the growing season, the wine produced can be sublime. The problem is the unpredictability of the weather, but this acuteness leads to much greater interest in the variations between individual vintages, which convey the weather patterns of that year in the final taste of the wine. Simply put, in Central Otago, in the years when it rains a lot the resultant wines tend to be watery and lack focus and concentration. You can really taste the weather in the wines of a marginal climate like Central Otago. It is the same in Burgundy and Bordeaux, where each year the style of the wine is different and reflects the weather patterns of the individual vintage. Just try comparing the 2010 and 2011 vintages in Bordeaux.

I drive up the South Island next towards Christchurch, the main city on the South Island. It has been sadly shattered by the effects of the powerful earthquake in 2011. A little further north I drive to the little-known area of Waipara, which I have heard has started producing some serious Pinot Noir wines. In fact, I helped make a Pinot Noir at one of the vineyards in this district a few years ago, so I'm aware of its potential. This first visit was rather random; I had heard on the "grapevine" that I should visit a winery called Fiddler's Green, where a winemaker was apparently making a delicious Pinot Noir in very small quantities. I veered off the main road and down another dirt track, at the end of which was a small, well-groomed vineyard. I was welcomed by Barry

Johns, a retired lawyer from Christchurch, who gave me a very good tasting. It is a family-run estate, established in 1993. The sheltered vineyards are on well-drained weathered limestone and gravel soils that Pinot Noir vines really enjoy. This small estate describes itself as *"the happy land imagined by sailors, where there is perpetual mirth, a fiddle that never stops playing for dancers who never tire..."* Barry uses sustainable vine-growing techniques which include minimal spraying, so the vines are more as nature intended. This translates into wines which are more free-range and have more character and flavour. I was very impressed with the Sauvignon Blanc here, which was less aggressive than most youthful Marlborough Sauvignons, more rounded and complex, and had an interesting hint of asparagus. I thought the Pinot Noir was outstanding, and, having bought the wine, I was delighted to see it being served in the first-glass cabin on Air New Zealand's international flights.

Marlborough was my next stop. It is right at the top of South Island, a much less marginal climate than Central Otago, so that there is more consistency in the final wines produced each year, despite being a maritime region. Led by the famous Cloudy Bay vineyard, the area is renowned for its Sauvignon Blancs, which are world-class. This was a triumph of marketing: the wine was originally only available on allocation to the trade, so all us wine traders would queue up for our twenty cases of the wine. Meanwhile, the consumer was desperate to get hold of it, as it came to be considered an iconic wine and only available in very small quantities. It now commands a high price, but is available in industrial quantities and distributed throughout the UK through supermarkets, restaurants and the independent wine trade too. To my mind the original Sauvignon Blanc blend, crafted by the talented winemaker Kevin Judd, with its hint of mid-palate ballast created through the subtle use of oak barrels for a small portion of the blend, displayed superior complexity to the volume blend of today. I think Cloudy Bay is still a smart product, but I'm not sure it is quite as good as it used to be when it was produced in much smaller quantities in the early 1990s. There are other Sauvignons from Marlborough which are very similar and less expensive. If you want a seriously good Sauvignon Blanc which is similar to Cloudy Bay and much less expensive, I would recommend Staete Landt Sauvignon Blanc in Marlborough, which is one of my favourites. Alternatively, I have shown Sauvignons from Sancerre and Pouilly-Fumé from the Loire valley of Northern France in a more marginal climate than Marlborough, but in comparison the best vintages will wipe the floor with anything from New Zealand. This is borne out in tutored wine tastings I have presented over the years, where the wines are tasted blind and a vote taken on which wine is preferred. Even the crisp dry Sauvignons from the cool Chilean climate of Casablanca, just north of the capital Santiago, are proving to be very good value indeed, even if they are not quite in the same league as Marlborough Sauvignons.

Marlborough is not just about Sauvignon, though. The region is also producing some stunning Chardonnays, which have been created using judicious levels of oak maturation, and which again are competing with the mid-range of village white Burgundies in France. Marlborough is also producing some really exceptional Pinot Noirs, mainly because the climate is sufficiently maritime and the cool sea breezes contribute to a generally not too hot or cold climate for this fastidious grape variety. The Staete Landt vineyard again makes a fine Pinot Noir, as does

Fromm, although Cloudy Bay makes an outstanding example at about twice the price. There are also some terrific Rieslings which, unusually for the New World, possess real focus, depth and grip, with a delightful concentration. These will mature well and only improve as the vines age further.

In 1995 I went to New Zealand on my honeymoon, hired a camper van and toured the North and South Islands. One day we found ourselves in Marlborough and, after a serious lunch at Alan Scott's vineyard restaurant, I introduced myself as someone from the British wine trade and was ushered up into his tasting room. Here, the winemaking team, including Alan himself, were huddled in the boardroom with lots of samples and glasses scattered all over the table. When I say boardroom, I mean the upstairs room above the hay barn.

Alan informed me that the team was trying to decide the blends for their *cuvées* from the previous year's vintage. I tasted through a series of wines, and Alan then asked me which wines I would blend together from the different plots on his extensive land. My wife patiently listened while I gave my view. The doctrine of holism, that the sum of the constituent parts proves superior to the plain individual singular parts, doesn't always work in wine. I believe that the French are right in their approach to *terroir*, and that often blending can lessen a wine. A wine produced from vines on a specific bit of land can sometimes reveal a pure, true individuality and identity which a blend cannot. There is something undeniably authentic about such a wine. Here in Marlborough, the blends under consideration were the different Sauvignon Blanc plants from different locations in the vineyard which had been vinified separately. Some of the grapes from the older vines on better sites had been fermented in barrel to add a texture and ballast to the mid-palate, emulating Kevin Judd's Cloudy Bay formula. I like a little barrel ageing in a Sauvignon Blanc, blended with some zippy, crisp, clean Sauvignon fruit cool-fermented in stainless steel. The longer cool fermentation protects and enhances the primary fruit aromas that give the wine its strong freshly cut grass and gooseberry nose. The combination of these two winemaking ingredients in the blend was a major factor in putting Cloudy Bay on the map. I concluded that the blend I would choose for their main blend should be a combination of these two facets, so that the overall taste of the wine would have this added complexity and interest. I was glad to hear that the winemaking team agreed with my conclusion and that was the blend for the 1995 vintage!

One of Alan's winemakers turned to my wife and asked, *"So is this business or pleasure for you, Nicola?"* My wife replied in a slightly exasperated way, *"This is my honeymoon."* The "moon" bit being quite high-pitched. The winemaker looked shocked.

Back to work, and Wellington is my next stop. First I drive to Picton, from where the ferry leaves to cross the Cook Strait, the narrow piece of water which connects North Island with South Island. It is named after James Cook, the first European commander to sail through it, in 1770. This treacherous stretch of water also connects the Tasman Sea on the north-west with the South Pacific Ocean on the south-east, and runs next to the capital city, Wellington. It is twenty-two kilometres wide at its narrowest point, and is considered one of the most dangerous and unpredictable waters in the world. I can vouch for that. On one occasion my crossing was incredibly rough.

I had my camera stolen from under my nose and didn't even notice, as I was rather more concerned and distracted by the waves crashing over the bow.

Back on dry land just outside Wellington on the North Island, I now discover that it is even more dangerous driving my car along a treacherous, narrow, windy road through the rugged mountains. I am ambushed by vertical hairpin bends with nothing to stop my car falling off the edge.

Finally I arrive in Martinborough, one of the most interesting and beautiful vineyard areas in New Zealand. This is not a place to confuse with Marlborough on South Island. It is much more spectacular and definitely worth the one-and-a-half-hour drive from Wellington. The long dry autumns in Martinborough finesse the flavours of the Pinot Noir, so that for me the finest Pinot Noirs in New Zealand are produced here. I drive straight on through Martinborough because I want to stay somewhere very special that no one knows about – it is a hidden gem, the most wonderful, characterful, authentic place you could imagine staying in, which dates back to 1919. The Lake Ferry Hotel is the oldest and southernmost hotel on the North Island. It is situated on the wild South Wairarapa coast, overlooking Cape Palliser and by the side of Lake Onoke, with huge mountains visible in the distance beyond the lake – a spectacular and beautiful spot. It's worth coming just to enjoy the views, but in addition, in my opinion, the finest, freshest fish in the world is served here with an unusually large number of wines served by the glass. I finally arrive just in time for supper – eating outside with the backdrop of this extraordinary landscape. It isn't expensive, it's certainly not ostentatious; I get my own bedroom but share a loo and a shower. It is just down to earth and should certainly be included in one of the *"20 places you have to visit before you die"*.

The following morning, I rise slightly bleary-eyed, having perhaps enjoyed a few too many wines by the glass the night before. I drive back towards Martinborough and discover the Basil Fawlty of the New Zealand wine world. Tim Coney and his wife Margaret decided to leave the big smoke of Wellington and take to the hills of Martinborough and plant a vineyard in their fifties. Tim had always lived on the edge as a foreign-exchange dealer, and he probably didn't realise life was going to get even more precarious. I am taken around Tim's well-tended vineyard here in Martinborough. It turns out his brother used to captain the New Zealand cricket team. I notice that his speech is fast, like a stream of consciousness, rather than structured with sentences and full stops. He spends five days a week toiling at gardening, as he calls it, in the vineyard, listening to music on his headphones and speaking to nobody. He clearly gets his own back on the other two days. The summer work involves pruning with clippers, "leaf-plucking" to give the grapes more exposure to the sun for better ripening, or training the vine to put its efforts into making berries rather than leaves. He then lets off steam at the weekends, when he can talk to people visiting the vineyard... like me. His descriptions of the wines demonstrate his talent as a wordsmith and his hyperactive imagination. For example, he describes his "Ragtime Riesling" as:

"The fifth infant in a line-up of deceitful trollops. Loose-limbed and precocious in her youth, this hussy, with her fructifying frankness, will render introverts garrulous within minutes of rounding the oesophagus. More objectively, her skirts hold promise of limes and lemons within. When clasped

in her succulent embrace, enthusiasts will stumble across honeysuckle and other alluring things. Drink up!"

That's wine for you!

I think the best and most expensive Pinot Noirs in New Zealand come from Martinborough, although the Marlborough Pinots are pretty close, if a little less expensive. In 1998, when I was studying for the Master of Wine exam, I wrote my thesis on a comparison of the Pinot Noirs in Martinborough with those in Burgundy, and concluded then that once the vines had aged a little more the quality of the Pinot Noirs would be as good if not better than the Grand Crus of Burgundy. I remember my tutor disagreeing vehemently with my prediction, although more recently I was delighted to read an article by the venerable Jancis Robinson MW taking a similar line in her *Financial Times* column.

Heading north, I find myself in Hawkes Bay. As I have driven north, so the climate has gradually become warmer. Hawkes Bay is certainly warm, and is the place to produce Cabernet Sauvignon and Merlot, with the equivalent of the Bordeaux climate in New Zealand. Here I visit the oldest vineyard in New Zealand, called Mission Estate, established on the famous Gimblett gravels in 1851. The soil is perfect for red-wine production, easily drained, and even the wines made from the Syrah grape have the focus, concentration and pepperiness that you expect in the finer wines of the northern Rhône.

The wines of New Zealand have improved considerably in recent years; the age of the vines is now getting to the point where some of the best wines can give the famous wines of Burgundy and the Loire a run for their money. The Sauvignons Blancs can be excellent, if a little obvious, the Pinot Noirs are now world-class, but the price of New Zealand wines has crept up, so careful selection is very important. There are definitely some outstanding jewels in the New Zealand cellar – supermodels, for sure.

"Wine lives and dies. It has not only its hot youth, strong maturity and weary dotage, but also its seasonal changes, its mysterious, almost mystical link with its parent vine, so that when the sap is running in the wood on the slopes of the Côte d'Or, in a thousand cellars, a thousand miles away the vine in its bottle quickens and responds."
Evelyn Waugh, New York *Vogue*, 1937

As the grape skin is crushed, so the natural yeasts on the outside of the grape skin mix with the sugar inside the grape and start a chemical reaction called fermentation, creating alcohol and carbon dioxide.

Once in the cellar it is the art and skill of the winemaker which is crucial in determining the character and quality of the final wine. You cannot make delicious wine from poor-quality grapes. That is impossible. You must have decent raw material in the first place. You can make poor-quality wine from quality grapes if, as a winemaker, you lack skill and understanding. The judgement of how to handle the grapes is critically significant.

In my experience the most atmospheric and characterful cellars are in Burgundy. Deep down in the ground, narrow stone corridors give way to larger, cavernous, dimly lit rooms with brick arches above rows of wooden casks lined up together, over which float cobwebs and a musty aroma. The only sound is the crunch of your shoes on the gravel floor – it's an eerie, exciting, different world down there.

There are lots of wonderful old cellars throughout France. In Saint-Émilion, further south near Bordeaux, and nestled on top of a hill, the town looks down over acres of vineyards, but underneath the surface soil of this hill there are catacombs of cellars. In one, at Château Pavie, the roots of a Merlot vine can be seen stretching through the ceiling of the cellar below, desperately seeking a drink. If the balloon goes up, you'll know where to find me.

So how can the winemaker use his talents to improve what nature has naturally provided? In warmer years more of the acidity in the grape is converted into sugar, which in turn will be turned into alcohol during the fermentation process. For white wines this could be damaging, so that the balance of the acidity in the final wine is out of kilter with the other elements. The wine could appear alcoholic, overweight, dumpy and soft, lacking in intensity, crispness and focus. It is not just winemakers in hot climates such as Australia who have the opportunity under these circumstances to "rectify" the blend by adding tartaric acid to increase the taste of acidity and sharpen the impression of the wine. If the acid is carefully and judiciously added, then the wine can be improved by the winemaker even in the cooler climate of northern

France. As a result of the unbelievably long, hot summer of 2003, some of the white wines in Mâcon were rectified to enhance the crispness and balance of the wines, which otherwise would have been soft and soupy. These practices may conceal "blemishes" at the surface level, but the fundamental balance of the wine will still be inadequate. A synthetic veneer may patch up the hollow taste of the wine, but it is not necessarily any substitute for real authentic quality and the genuine natural beauty of a wine made in a great vintage where the weather was perfect – such as Bordeaux in 2009.

Equally, in a cool climate in some vintages there is not enough warmth and sunshine to ripen the grapes fully. The grapes will lack sugar, so that the final wine, if left to nature, will be lacking in alcohol, roundness and balance, with too severe an acidity, which may taste green, unripe and bitter. Under strict regulations, a winemaker in northern Europe is allowed to add sugar into the brew of unfermented grape juice so as to increase the alcohol and weight of the final wine. This is an attempt through the winemaking process to improve what nature has naturally provided. It is sometimes called enrichment, and as a method to improve wine it has a long history – even the Romans used to do it by adding honey.

The winemaker can thus have a profound effect and, by using a sort of cosmetic surgery on the juice in the cellar, can turn an average wine into something potentially much better.

As my mother-in-law likes to say:

"Men are like fine wine: they all start out like grapes, and it's a woman's job to stomp all over them and crush them in the dark until they mature into something you'd like to have dinner with."

The true character of a red wine, as discussed earlier, is determined by the length of time the red grape skins are left in contact with the juice in the vat. Given the right amount of time, the fruit tannin will be in balance. Too brief and not enough character is extracted; too long and the fruit tends to taste stewed and astringent, and the wine will not be in balance. A useful method of extracting plenty of colour while not extracting tannin is a type of winemaking called carbonic maceration. This is a technique where whole unblemished grapes are fermented in the vat under a blanket of carbon dioxide prior to crushing. Wines created using this method are ready to drink much earlier, because there is so little tannin and they will not age for long. It's a method of winemaking which is used in Beaujolais, for those immensely vibrant fruity wines: the drawback is that complexity does not tend to be included as one of their hallmarks.

How much oak influence do you give the wine? Do you leave the wine in expensive oak casks to provide reds with a chocolatey, oaky, spicy, smoky flavour with additional oak tannins? Alternatively, do you ferment the wine in temperature-controlled stainless-steel vats where the fruit flavour will be more piercingly apparent and the aromas of the grape more evident in the final wine? If the temperature of fermentation is kept down during the fermentation of a red wine, it will increase the length of that fermentation and make it a more gradual, slower process. In so doing the primary fruit aromas will be preserved in the final wine, so that when you pour the wine into your glass and sink your nose in, the power and intensity of that smell relates directly back to the coolness of the fermentation. Equally, if the winemaker allows the yeasts a free rein to do as they like in a perfectly natural fermentation – in barrel, for example – the temperature will rise as the yeasts enjoy a frenzy of activity, gorging themselves on the sugars while the heat rises. Under these circumstances, the final wine tends to be a little more rich, smooth and rounded, but the nose will be mute and there will be little evidence of those vibrant primary fruit aromas. It is, as so often in winemaking and in life, a matter of balance.

In white wines, Chardonnays in particular, maturing the wine in new oak will provide that delicious honeyed, vanilla, butterscotch and caramel bouquet, together with a buttery taste and a deeper yellow colour in the wine. The oak will add complexity, but its addition should be carefully judged. A superb-quality white wine such as Chablis Premier Cru from the cool climate of northern France is also made from the Chardonnay grape. It usually isn't held in oak casks at all, but instead demonstrates its quality in the refined, restrained intensity, purity and mineral concentration that these great wines display. This natural style is enhanced by a delightful persistent lingering flavour in the mouth once you've swallowed the wine. Premier Cru Chablis is considered "fine" because of its purity and the fact that it has not been matured in new French oak barrels to add unneeded complexity. This is not considered a deficit in its character, but an enhancement. In fact, winemakers sometimes want to increase this searing natural crisp acidity in white wines by blocking the second natural fermentation which happens after the first. This is called the malolactic fermentation, and is the conversion of harsh malic acids (which tend to taste of green apples) into softer, more rounded lactic acids, which taste richer and more buttery. It is carried out by the family of lactic acid bacteria. This gives the final wine more breadth and a fuller, softer "mouthfeel" on the palate.

By blocking this chemical reaction, the intensity and crispness in the final wine can be controlled and enhanced if that is a character which the winemaker wants to preserve. These characteristics are certainly beneficial in a white wine which is designed to go with rich foods, as the acidity will cut through the fattiness and enhance the taste experience. Raw smoked salmon or fish cooked in a rich, creamy or cheesy sauce are a delight with a wine, like a Chablis Premier Cru, with serious acidity. In a really hot climate, searing acidity in a wine will taste refreshing and thirst-quenching on its own. The winemaker should certainly consider the market and clients for whom his wine is destined.

The longer the red grape skins are left stewing in the vat or cask during and after the fermentation has taken place, the more deep red colour and the more tannin will be produced in the final red wine. The tannin's other function is to preserve the wine and provide its ability to age.

Conversely, for white wine, the grapes are pressed and the grape skins are generally taken away swiftly, and here it is the acidity in the grape which preserves the wine in the shorter term. Sometimes a winemaker will leave the lees, or the remains of the grape skins, in the barrel for longer and give them a stir regularly to impart a little more character and flavour into the wine. An example of this is in the well-known wine called Muscadet produced in the Loire Valley, close to the sea at Nantes. In this maritime climate, not surprisingly, the wine has always been produced to go with fish and, in particular, shellfish. The grape variety used to make Muscadet is the Melon de Bourgogne, which has a searing acidity. It is almost translucent in its appearance, and on a hot summer's day in France is the perfect wine to go with the famous French dish *"plateau de fruits de mer"*, a dish which contains all sorts of different shellfish, including lobster, crab, shrimp and mussels, all served on a huge platter, which you normally share. This lunch is delicious served with a bottle of Muscadet, preferably *"sur lie"*, which is normally advertised on the bottle and is a step up from the basic Muscadet and worth the minimal extra cost.

I have a very happy memory of spending an afternoon on holiday in France enjoying just such a lunch in the Loire valley. The only problem is that after you have taken two hours to work painstakingly to extract the fish flesh from all those different shells, you're still absolutely starving!

The Muscadet winemaker has produced a wine, however, that goes perfectly with shellfish, by stirring the lees and blocking the malolactic fermentation to enhance your sizzling and tingling tasting experience.

For quality rosé, the red grape skins are left in the vat for a very brief period, normally less than twenty-four hours, to extract a little pink colour. The best rosés, in my opinion, are the subtle salmon-pink ones that are lighter in colour and alcohol. Too many rosés these days can be almost red in colour and too high in alcohol. For me the alcohol should be less than 13% – preferably 12 to 12.5%. Decent rosé needs a cool climate so that the acidity is naturally crisp and the alcohol is naturally low. Too often the alcohol can be too high, the delicious primary fruit aromas of wild strawberries can be subdued and the alcohol overpowering. What is more, some winemakers cheat and make a poor-quality rosé by just mixing a red and a white wine together.

As Evelyn Waugh intimated earlier, during the fermentation the wine does get hot – rising in temperature to more than 35 degrees if left naturally bubbling away. In a rosé wine this would be a disaster. Most fermentations are cooled to some extent so the wine is not allowed to get too hot, and therefore to preserve the more subtle aromas in the wine.

Wine is a living being; it develops and matures over time and finally dies as it turns into vinegar.

So how long should you cellar wine? How long will it last?

The stock response to this question is: *"In my house about twenty minutes."* For me, wine improves with age... I like it more the older I get!

The general rule of thumb as to when to drink wine is: the better and more expensive the wine, the longer it should last. Furthermore, some grape varieties last longer than others in bottle, mainly because of the tannin in the wine. Red Bordeaux generally keeps longer than Burgundy. A top-quality Bordeaux will keep for more than thirty years (the Cabernet Sauvignon in Bordeaux is a more robust, thicker-skinned grape variety producing more tannin and longevity than the thinner-skinned Pinot Noir). Except for sweet and exceptionally good white wine, whites should be drunk within a few years of the vintage and generally don't improve with laying down for any significant period. The very top white wines of the Côte de Beaune in Burgundy, such as Corton-Charlemagne, Meursault, Puligny and Chassagne-Montrachet, can be kept for ten years or more and in their youth can taste lean and acidic, but as they age a wonderful honeyed complexity emerges. The expensive white wine Condrieu, from the northern Rhône, is another exception to the rule. It is produced in small quantities from the village of the same name, and made entirely from the Viognier grape. This very fine wine needs time to develop its complexity. Even expensive Sauvignons Blancs from other parts of the world, such as Cloudy Bay, Baron de L Pouilly-Fumé, Sancerre and Edwards Sauvignon Blanc from the Margaret River region of Western Australia, need a few years after the vintage to lose their sharp acidic crispness and show a little less of their attention-seeking youthful exuberance. On a very hot summer's day, the acidity in a white wine tastes refreshing rather than lean, so even very young Sauvignons can, in the heat of the midday sun, be drunk young.

The other great white wine which can be kept longer, and should be, is Riesling. It always used to be considered the greatest of the white grapes emanating from northern Germany along the banks of the Rhine and Mosel, with some of the best coming from nearby Alsace. Now terrific Rieslings are made all over the world, although the best ones are generally from cool climates. It is worth noting that since Riesling has lost some of its popularity to the better known and understood Chardonnay and Sauvignon Blanc varieties, very often Riesling will provide much better value for money.

As a wine ages, so it moves from its initial primary fruit character into the secondary phase, when the fruit in a red wine is gradually broken down through oxidation, ageing into more vegetal flavours. For me the best time to drink red wines is when they still retain a little of the fruit but there are also some of those secondary flavours such as truffles, leather, coffee, chocolate and tobacco coming through in a complex delicious harmony. Often, and this is particularly true of Pinot

Noir, the wine will go into a "mute" phase between the end of primary fruit and the secondary development, when there is very little flavour, aroma or taste – but wait a year or so and these flavours will return.

So wine is a living being: it develops from its initial simple fruitiness and finally dies as the fruit disintegrates and a tawny colour degenerates into vinegar. But as the years pass and as a wine develops in the bottle, rather like some human beings, it matures and becomes more complex and interesting, with many more intriguing stories to tell.

Without the advice of a reputable wine merchant, how do you know when to drink a fine red wine? First off, I would recommend buying a case of twelve bottles preferably *en primeur*, as generally this will give you the best value for money. This means buying the wine before it has been bottled and taking delivery – if you have a cellar at home – about three years after the vintage. Alternatively, you can keep it in bond with a merchant, whilst paying an annual storage charge. It is then sensible to try a single bottle from the case and see what it tastes like. If it's still bright purple, really tannic and acidic and hard and mean, clearly it needs time. If it's going brown at the rim and the core of your glass, and the fruit has dried out in an oxidised tannic roughness, then it is too old to drink. If a wine is too young you can help it age a little by putting it into a jug to breathe in the oxygen and develop more quickly before putting it in your glass. The best time to drink a wine is when the fruit is still there but it is starting to develop some secondary flavours and more complexity. The fruit is soft and appealingly open and intense, but there is more depth to the wine beyond and behind those compelling flavours, telling of further intricacies and a hugely satisfying long and lingering finish. The balance of the fruit, alcohol, tannin and acidity are all aligned and beautifully harmonious. A wine which is too young will have too much tannin and acidity. A wine which is too old will have too little fruit and vitality. As a lady who owned a French vineyard once said to me, the perfectly aged fine wine, which we should all strive to discover, *"is like having an orgasm in the mouth"*.

There are many of us who unfortunately do not possess a cellar, so where should you keep your wine? The first thing is don't leave it in a rack in the kitchen, however splendid-looking the rack is. In the kitchen the temperature goes up and down rapidly and frequently, and this is death to wine.

The most important thing when storing wine, is to keep the temperature stable, ideally at 10 degrees Celsius. The bottles need to be kept on their sides so the wine is constantly in contact with the cork. The danger if the bottles are left standing up is that the corks will dry out. If the cork dries out it will not perform the function for which it was designed, which is to prevent air getting into the wine. In these circumstances the wine may become oxidised and musty. Wine should also be stored away from direct sunlight, which can damage it. So the sensible place in the house to store wine is away from radiators in an area where the temperature is as constant as possible.

You could have a "spiral cellar", a special hole with a staircase to store your wine under the ground, but these can be expensive. The best place to store wine in my experience is often under the stairs in the middle of the house. In general, the warmer the constant temperature is, the faster your wine will mature, and if the wine is held in a cooler temperature this will slow down its development.

There is the story of a man who was storing wine all over his house and one day his wife, who had had enough, ordered him to pour it all down the sink:

"I had 36 bottles of wine scattered about my house, which had spread even as far as the shower. I was told by my erstwhile wife to empty them down the sink – or else. I said I would and proceeded with the unpleasant task. I drew the cork from the first bottle and poured the contents down the sink, with the exception of one glass, which I drank.

With the second I did likewise.

I then drew the cork from the third bottle and poured the wine down the sink, which I drank.

I pulled the cork from the fourth bottle down the sink and poured the bottle down the glass, which I drank.

I fool so feelish.

I pulled the bottle from the cork of the next and drank one sink of it and threw the next down the glass, which I drank.

I poured the sink out of the next glass and poured the cork down the bottle.

Then I corked the drunk with the glass, bottled the drink and drank the pour. When I had everything empty I steadied the house with one hand, counted the glasses, corks bottles, sinks, which with the others were 45.

As the house came by I counted them again and finally had all the houses in one bottle, which I drank.

I am not under the affluence of incahol as thinkle peep I am. I am not half as think as you might drunk. In fact I fool so feelish I don't know who is me and the drunker I stand the longer I get."

The other alternative is to buy a large cellar with a small house on top.

In conclusion, the winemaker has an important and profound impact on the style and character of the final wine. Techniques are used to improve the natural weather-derived characteristics of different wines, to conceal the deficiencies of nature and enhance the balance of the components of the final wine.

The finest wines are those where the winemaker is not required to compensate, add or subtract anything from the wine, as the grapes are perfectly ripe and in balance. The real, authentic, intrinsic quality and breeding in a wine is derived from the climate and the weather of each individual vintage. The winemaker would prefer to interfere as little as possible in the cellar during this extraordinary natural process of converting the grapes into wine. The cellar should play host to the natural beauty of the winemaker's creation, rather than interfering with cosmetic surgery. Unfortunately, we don't live in a utopia where every year the weather is perfect and the grapes are always grown in perfect weather conditions.

"With wine in hand, one reaches the happy state – where men are wise, women beautiful; and even one's children begin to look promising."
Anon.

Another beautiful setting for vineyards is in the Cape Winelands of South Africa. Enormous mountains and granite outcrops tower over the vineyards' spectacular view of the Atlantic Ocean meeting the Indian Ocean only a short distance from the rocky coast.

I asked my PA to organise the cheapest hire car she could find, and she obviously took me at my word. I was given an ancient Volkswagen which had no air conditioning, no assisted steering – in fact, no assisted anything. Just turning the wheel provided a considerable workout in the 40° C heat, so unfortunately I would arrive at each appointment completely shattered and looking as though I had just returned from the gym.

The vineyards of the Cape have the usual mix of interesting wildlife with which to share their crop. Some vineyards in South Africa have problems with impatient baboons, who prefer to eat ripe Pinot Noir grapes directly from the vine rather than having the tiresome and lengthy wait until after fermentation.

Cape leopards used to patrol the vine rows deterring the baboons from coming into the vineyard, but leopards are now in short supply, so the baboons have grown more confident in South Africa. One winemaker told me the story of a troop of about forty baboons invading his Pinot Noir vineyard and stealing his crop in Elgin just outside Cape Town. (Incidentally, I discovered why Cape Town is known as the "Mother City" of South Africa: it is because it takes nine months to get anything done there.)

The viticulturist was sent off for the first time to frighten them away. He began by throwing stones at them and repeatedly shouting "shoo". The rest of the curious winery staff arrived later to help him out, only to discover the poor fellow, battered and bruised, cowering defensively behind his car. All had gone well until the baboons had thought it rather a good game to hurl the stones back at him. At least this vineyard manager could do something about the invasion of his vineyard: a *vigneron* in the Languedoc in France woke up one morning at the beginning of October, intending to start picking his grapes that day, only to discover that during the night thieves had stolen his entire crop using two very efficient mechanical harvesters.

The Cape cobra is another creature that lurks amidst the vines of South Africa. This snake is rarely seen, as it likes to slither by itself in a Rudyard Kipling sort of way, enjoying its own company. This is in contrast to the puff adder, another more lazy snake often found amongst the vines, which moves for nobody, so if you happen to interrupt its sunbathing it will attack you, sink its fangs deep into your ankle and wrap itself around you at the same time.

The climate of the Cape is warm, despite the sea breezes, and the renowned "Cape Doctor", the constant wind (much like the mistral in the southern Rhône valley), is known for its ability to dry out the vines after rain to prevent mildew and disease from infecting the grapes. The wind is also important in slowing down the ripening process by keeping the grapes cool and preventing them from overheating.

Every 10 km one travels inland, the temperature rises by half a degree. Equally for every 100 metres you climb, the temperature falls by half a degree. I am therefore exploring the higher vineyards close to the sea and preferably on the cooler south-facing slopes – the mirror image of those north of the equator. Here I hope to find more elegant wines with greater intensity and aroma derived from the lower temperatures. The genuinely cooler vineyard areas in South Africa are the higher parts of Stellenbosch, Durbanville, Elgin, Walker Bay and, of course, Constantia, where vine-growing in the Cape was introduced in the 1660s. Today the two finest Pinot Noirs in South Africa come from Walker Bay: Hamilton Russell and Bouchard Finlayson, both vineyards close to the sea, produce excellent wines. Meerlust, which is hotter, is also interesting in that it produces a delicious Pinot, proving that, even in climates which are considered too hot, there are cooler micro-climates that benefit from height or wind, or both, to produce world-class wines from fastidious grapes, such as Pinot Noir.

In the hot climates of the Southern Hemisphere, vineyards are generally situated near the sea and reasonably high up, otherwise the climate is just too hot to create fine wine. It's not just during fermentation when grapes can heat up too much and then destroy the subtle primary fruit aromas; the same thing can happen before harvest naturally if the vineyard is too hot and the grapes are burnt in the intense sunshine.

There is one vineyard in Franschhoek, a gastronomic as well as vinous centre not far from Stellenbosch, where an ancient avocado tree stood close to the winery. The owner had two Alsatians, which seemed to be uninterested in me when I arrived and snoozed lazily under the shadow of the tree. These two ferocious-looking dogs had discovered, I was told, that when the avocados dropped with a thud onto the ground they were perfectly ripe and ready to eat. Whenever the avocados fell with a bang there was a moment of calm as the two Alsatians regarded each other surreptitiously out of the corner of their eyes. The winemaker would also look at the Alsatians. The Alsatians would regard the winemaker, pretending to be uninterested, and then look intently at their master, until eventually one of them could resist no more and would scamper forward, paws raking the earth, rushing for the avocado that was now lying on the ground. There would then be a mad frantic race amidst a cloud of dust to see which animal could beat the winemaker to the fruit first.

While in Franschhoek, you must visit Reuben's restaurant in the high street on the left as you head towards the Huguenot Memorial; it is superb, and I have enjoyed my finest meals in South Africa there.

The South African wine industry was held back during the years of apartheid, when trade sanctions were imposed. Now it is beginning to catch up with the rest of the wine world, as more investment is directed into the vineyards. To me, the best wines of South Africa now offer the rich juicy fruit of the New World coupled with the spiciness, elegance, minerality and subtlety of the old world. It can be the best of both worlds in your glass. Mooiplaas Vineyard is my favourite spot in Stellenbosch. Mooiplaas means "beautiful place", and this vineyard certainly is. As high as 380 metres above sea level the vineyard is cool at night and the view of Table Mountain, the Atlantic Ocean and Cape Town in the distance is spectacular. The vineyard was established in 1963 and is now run by Louis Roos and his brother, who are the second generation to make wine here. The wines are elegant and aromatic, and the Pinotage is the best I have ever tasted. The problem with Pinotage is that there is an awful lot of it that is really not very interesting at all – a sort of cross between a cheap French table wine and Beaujolais Nouveau. It is in fact a 1925 cross between Pinot Noir and Cinsaut created by Abraham Perold at Stellenbosch University. In those days the Cinsaut was known as Hermitage, hence the name Pinotage.

There is the story of an Englishman, an Aussie and a South African who are in a bar one night. All of a sudden the South African downs his wine, throws his glass in the air, pulls out a gun, shoots the glass to pieces and says: *"In Sath Efrika our glasses are so cheap that we don't need to drink from the same one twice."* The Aussie, obviously impressed by this, drinks his wine, throws his glass into the air, pulls out his gun, shoots the glass to pieces and says: *"Well, mate, in Straaaaaaaaaaaaailia we have so much sand to make the glasses that we don't need to drink out of the same glass twice either."* The Englishman, cool as a cucumber, picks up his wine, drinks it, throws his glass into the air, pulls out the gun, shoots the South African and the Australian and then says: *"In London we have so many South Africans and Australians that we don't need to drink with the same ones twice."*

On my last day in South Africa I managed to find time to dive with great white sharks off the Cape. A giant old fetid bloody fish head is dropped over the side of the boat into the choppy waters, and then it is just a matter of time and waiting for the man-eaters to arrive. I waited for about an hour before two great whites suddenly appeared as large dark moving shadows under the boat. Then their fins appeared in that menacing way above the water circling our boat. Memories of the whole audience screaming in the cinema watching the film *Jaws* suddenly returned, as our captain put a steel cage over the side of the boat in the path of these two menacing fish. I didn't think anyone would be silly enough to get into the cage, but to my surprise and concern everyone apart from me, the token Brit, was volunteering to put on a wetsuit. I enquired whether there were any chain-mail suits and was given short shrift. After everyone except me had slipped into the cage to have a closer look beneath the boat, peer pressure took its toll and I jumped into the water. Jaws arrived to have a closer look at me and swam past inches from the cage, and I looked closely into its dark, cold-blooded, emotionless, killer eyes. There's only one other place I've witnessed those eyes before, although I haven't been to a firm of lawyers for some time. I gather the answer to why sharks do not attack lawyers is… professional courtesy!

Another visit in Stellenbosch, and I arrive at the Boschkloof vineyard. (The name literally means "little valley of bushes".)

One good thing about meeting winemakers is they don't spin a story about the wine: they tell you why it tastes the way it does and fully answer follow-up questions rather than just giving you the marketing spiel. So often in France you ask the thirteenth generation of winemaker why the wine is made in this way, and their response is… *"because my father made wine like this and my grandfather made wine in the same way and I am continuing the family tradition".*

However, in South Africa, if you ask a winemaker the same question the answer will be a detailed analysis of the consequences of those actions and why this helps to make the wine taste better.

In South Africa there is an esteemed group of winemakers called the Cape Winemakers Guild. This select body of 39 members are leaders in the art of winemaking there. Potential members are only invited if they have been responsible for producing outstanding wines for a minimum of five years, and they must continue to produce excellence to remain members of the Guild, guaranteeing an enduring association of top-end wine producers. One member of the Guild is Jacques Borman, who has over thirty years' experience as a winemaker, having spent over twenty years at La Motte and Chamonix in Franschhoek.

(The Chamonix winery is another brilliant place to have lunch, as the winery's restaurant is situated high up, overlooking the valley; both the food and the view are magnificent and you can eat outside in a shady spot.)

Jacques makes the wine at this small vineyard called Boschkloof, which I discovered on my visit to South Africa in 2007. I returned to his winery more recently and tasted a selection of his wines again, and was truly impressed with the quality he is producing. On each label there is a picture of the Holy Grail chalice, and Jacques Borman's motto is *inconcessum persequor* ("I pursue the unattainable"), which, in his view, is creating the perfect wine – surely an impossibility, but as a proud member of the Guild he is still striving hard. As Robert Louis Stevenson said, *"Sometimes it is better to travel hopefully than to arrive."*

Jacques is one of the most talented winemakers I have met, coaxing so much more out of the grapes – something which is reflected in the final characterful wine. It is here that I discover the wines which combine the intense concentrated rich fruit of the New World with the structure, minerality, restraint and subtlety of the Old. The Boschkloof Syrah is a good example. It has the spice and pepper on the nose of a northern Rhône Syrah, but then when you taste it the richness of the sweet, ripe, intense fruit is more assertive than you would find in many an expensive northern Rhône wine. Their Merlot has a similar mix, with juicy blackcurrant fruit character balanced with firm, spicy, toasted tannins and a long, lingering, forceful finish. This again is just what I am looking for – wines which are almost as good as the top wines, but at a fraction of the cost.

A relatively new and exciting vineyard area in the Cape is Elgin. It is cool and high and looks as though in due course it will produce some excellent Pinot Noir. Currently it is producing mainly white wines, but the vineyards are young and the wines lack depth. I stumbled across an excellent Cap Classique from this area made by Ross Gower. These sparkling wines are made in the same way as champagne. I came across a superb rosé Cap Classique "fizz" made from 100% Pinot Noir. It was rich, biscuity and delicious, and it reminded me a little of a top Grande Marque which has had time to develop in bottle. Ross was a giant of a man, and has spent twenty years being the winemaker at Klein Constantia, but has now set up on his own with his two sons. I went back to see him recently to discover a very thin, frail man, who looked much older. He had been diagnosed with cancer and looked ravaged by the illness, although he was still making the wine and fighting the cancer.

Exploring vineyards in South Africa is much safer, despite the snakes and sharks. It is on the hills and mountains, where the altitude, the slope and the aspect contribute to the *terroir*, producing the right conditions where the vines can flourish, as they are well drained, whilst in the full glare of the not too hot sun. The finest wines around the world are generally produced on a slope, whether it is looking down the steep banks of the Mosel in Germany, high up on the hill of Hermitage in the Rhône, the foothills of the Andes mountains in Chile and Argentina or on the gently sloping east-facing hills of the Côte d'Or in Burgundy. The resultant nectar is concentrated with an intensity to delight the taste buds.

One problem for South African winemakers is to decide where they fit into the global wine world and what it is about South African wine which makes it so special. In Argentina the exports of Malbec are growing fast. In Chile there is the Merlot, together with some outstandingly huge brands which are exporting increasingly to North America. In New Zealand Sauvignon Blanc, Pinot Noir and more expensive wines are finding a home in the global market. Australia has their amazingly fruit-powered Shiraz and the iconic Penfolds. What should South Africa focus on? Pinotage, which is its calling card, is never in my view going to be a world-beater; the quality is simply just not there. Steen, or Sauvignon Blanc, is not ideally suited to the heat of South Africa, and it will never be an "icon" wine. In my view, the way ahead for South African wines is with Syrah and Cabernet Sauvignon. It is grown at higher altitude and enjoys that unique balance of rich ripe fruit, coupled with the complexity found in French wines from Bordeaux and the Rhône Valley. If the South Africans can market themselves as the best of both worlds, allow their vines to grow older and keep their prices reasonable, the future for their wines is exciting.

On the aeroplane back to the UK, as we fly over Tanzania, I begin to doze, and memories of a previous African expedition to climb Mount Kilimanjaro, the highest mountain in Africa and the highest free-standing mountain in the world, come flooding back. I wanted to raise money for the charity Help for Heroes, which does so much for wounded servicemen and women returning from battle. Here are the notes from my diary of the final summit ascent.

'We left for the final assault on the summit just before midnight on 14th January. It was a beautifully bright, starlit clear night. The 12 of us set off from Kibu Hut at 16,000 ft above sea level, with head torches darting a stream of light into the quiet eerie darkness, as we ascended 'pole-pole' (slowly slowly) in single file. Nobody in our group had climbed to this height before, so no one was quite sure how the altitude would affect them. First climbed in 1889 by Hans Meyer, only 40% of the people who attempt 'Kili' each year reach the summit. It soon became apparent why as, after an hour, we split into three or four groups to alter the pace to cater for those struggling. Sickness, nausea, light-headedness and the freezing cold eventually played varying amounts of havoc on us all. I think I was wearing about nine layers, but to begin with it wasn't excessively cold.

"We trudged up, with the path becoming steeper and more shingly, my boots slipping sideways down the hill as we zigzagged up the mountain. As we neared Gilman's Point on the crater rim, the route became very steep and rocky and we scrambled on all fours. It was at this point, with the temperature at minus 15 degrees and feelings of nausea overcoming my body, that I began to question whether I would make it, unsteady as I was on my feet, with my legs shaking uncontrollably.

"And then suddenly there was Gilman's Point, the crater rim, at over 18,700 ft. The sun was just beginning to show its face as we walked along the crater rim towards Uhuru (which means 'freedom' in Swahili), the summit. The sun shone across from a brilliant blue and red sky, casting shadows of our bodies to the side of us on the snow as we moved on past the glacier of memorable beauty. Eventually, after another hour, at 7.09 a.m., I made it to the summit at 19,341 ft. I felt in my trouser pocket for the hip flask of Malbec from Argentina which I had carefully carried all the way up, and poured it with trembling hands into a glass from my backpack. It was body temperature, absolutely perfect. I raised this glass of exceedingly good Malbec to our wounded heroes returning home and shared it as a loving cup with my comrades who had also made it to the roof of Africa. I certainly needed another glass at the end of the 16-hour marathon!"

On another occasion, still in Africa, after finishing university, I remember attempting to climb one of the pyramids in Giza, close to the Sphinx, in Egypt. Three of my party decided that going around the back into the shadows behind the pyramids during the *son et lumière* would give us cover to carry out this illegal activity. We wanted to open a bottle on the top of the pyramid, toast the Sphinx and sleep the night there under the stars.

We crept round in the shadows to the dark side of the pyramid and started to climb. At about 250 metres up I realized that not only was the slope becoming much steeper, but in addition the steps to heave oneself up had disappeared through the onslaught of the wind and rain over thousands of years, and had now degenerated into a steep, flat, shingly surface, down which I was extremely likely to slip. I discovered later that a few people are killed every year attempting to climb this pyramid, which is why the bottom has now been cordoned off with barbed wire to prevent people from trying it. Worse still, I was carrying a large plastic bag with my sleeping bag and various iron rations in one hand just to make the whole climb a little more challenging. As I grabbed nervously at a stone to hold on to, the stone came away in my hand and I lurched backwards, thinking in that split second that this was the end and I would now fall to my certain death. Incredibly, somehow my body didn't move and the stone under my right foot held firm. I stopped to think, and decided that if I moved to the side, to the corner of the pyramid, I was more likely to find the steps in the rock to provide a safer route to the top. I moved to the corner and, sure enough, the big steps were there, and gradually I made it up to the top in the darkness. The view from the top towards the Sphinx, lit up with spotlights below us, was magical. Unfortunately I had broken the bottle on the way up, and the following morning there was a reception committee waiting for us at the bottom demanding baksheesh.

A good view from a height is always a pleasure and makes the climb worthwhile. It is also true that grapes grown at a decent altitude in a warm climate will generally produce wines which are more exciting and elegant than the wines produced at lower altitudes in the heat.

"Entertaining a guest means you take charge of their happiness for the whole time he or she is with you. What better way to treat a guest than to drink wine together slowly and with friends."
Henry McNulty, *Vogue A-Z of Wine*

A publishing friend of mine once told me that he had to take out a famous author one evening with his wife and various important clients to a smart restaurant in London. A lot of money rested on the success of this relationship, so he wanted to make sure that the impression he gave as a host was a good one. He ordered a white wine to go with a fishy starter, to which the wine waiter replied, *"Are you sure you want to order that wine?"* It was one of those acutely embarrassing moments of which I increasingly realise life is full. The host was trying to look knowledgeable and full of *savoir faire*, but succeeded in achieving the reverse. *"What's wrong with the wine? Is it not one you would recommend?"*

"Well no, not really, not with fish, you see, sir, it's sweet." The poor fellow put a brave face on, but since life is all about perception, his reputation was sunk in his glass. The publishing contract went to someone else.

So what should you do when wishing to impress colleagues, staff or clients in a smart restaurant? Firstly, don't select the second wine down on the white or the red wine list, as it is the wine that enormous numbers of wine novices choose, because they don't want to spend too much on a bottle, but they also don't want to select the cheapest wine either.

Restaurant owners are aware of this and sometimes the wine is actually less expensive to buy in than the cheapest wine but the price is raised, because the owner of the restaurant knows perfectly well that this will be the most popular wine, so he organises a bigger profit on it.

One of my friends has been entertaining corporately for many years in the City of London, and often the clients are worth millions of pounds to the company. For him it is very important that the impression he gives is one of quiet, polished, understated sophistication. He doesn't want to go for the most expensive wine, as that would seem profligate, but equally he doesn't want to go for the least expensive wine either, as that would seem mean and would undervalue the client.

Somewhere on a wine list, below the two cheapest wines, there is an ideal wine which is the perfect choice. My friend sometimes takes the trouble to email the restaurant wine list to me beforehand and to ask my advice as to which wines he should choose to go with a particular menu he has already decided upon. As the old army saying goes, *"Time spent on reconnaissance is seldom wasted."* Planning and preparation, as in so many things in life, is crucial. As my father used to say, *"If you fail to plan, you plan to fail!"*

93

Many wine lists are now online, so an early viewing could help. My recommendation is, if you are not sure what to start with, order a bottle of house fizz, or if the budget is there one of the Grande Marque champagnes, as in my experience this gets a celebration off to a fine start. The bubbles in champagne force the alcohol into the bloodstream more swiftly, so any initial social tension disappears more quickly too. If it is a more low-key affair in the middle of summer, perhaps eating out on a terrace, I like a glass of rosé.

A special French wine cocktail which my wife has taken to with alacrity is a Kir Royal, which is a mixture of fizz (I wouldn't waste champagne on this drink) and a thimbleful of the liqueur *crème de cassis*. The important thing is to ensure that there is just a hint of *cassis* and the colour of the cocktail is salmon pink, pale and interesting. 1/10 would be my recipe. Otherwise, if it is a deep-red colour, you lose the subtlety and balance in the blend.

Alternatively the French are very partial to a straight Kir, which is white wine mixed with *crème de cassis*. Traditionally this was made using Bourgogne Aligoté, as the white wine has a distinctly fresh acidity and blends rather well with the richness and sweetness of the liqueur. Nowadays restaurants tend to mix a Kir with any white wine which they have lying around, and in truth most less expensive white wines with a decent level of acidity will mix well for a Kir cocktail. There are some old-fashioned people who believe that this is like Buck's Fizz: it ruins two perfectly good drinks by mixing them together.

The story of the origin of Kir is an interesting one. Monsieur Kir was mayor of Dijon during the Second World War. At the time of the occupation, he was considered rather correct, and even possibly a sympathiser with the Germans, until 1944, when it was discovered, to the complete surprise of everyone, that he was the leader of the French resistance in the Dijon region. The Germans were shocked at being outmanoeuvred by this courageous man and sent a hit squad to Dijon and shot Monsieur Kir from a passing car in one of the back streets. A member of the family of one of my Burgundy suppliers found him and took him immediately to the local hospital, and thanks to his quick thinking saved his life. So every time we raise a glass of Kir we are raising it to a very brave leader of the French resistance.

If you are not sure about the first wine to order in a restaurant, I would recommend asking the wine waiter or the sommelier for advice. He is, after all, the professional. Does the restaurant have a particular white wine which could be recommended to go with whatever starter many in the group have chosen?

Otherwise the banker for a starter is a dry white Burgundy. Made from the Chardonnay grape, this wine will go virtually with any first course. If you want something a little less expensive, Bourgogne Blanc is the entry-level white Burgundy, and in my view always a pretty reliable wine that should be of good quality and reasonably priced. You could choose a Sauvignon Blanc, which has a higher acidity and also goes pretty well with any starter. A classy alternative option is to choose a Pouilly-Fumé from the Loire Valley. A dry Vouvray made from the Chenin Blanc grape variety is also a terrific accompaniment to a mildly spicy starter. If money is no object and it is a special occasion a top-class white Burgundy would be my selection – a Puligny-Montrachet, Chassagne-Montrachet or Meursault.

The alternative is to choose a less expensive New World option such as a Sauvignon from Casablanca in Chile or a Sauvignon from New Zealand or the cooler climes of Australia, perhaps Margaret River. You could do worse than select an inexpensive Bordeaux Sauvignon, which tends to be better value than a Loire Sauvignon such as Cuvée Clémence from the Entre-Deux-Mers region, which is a delightful traditional dry Bordeaux blend of Sauvignon Blanc, Sémillon and Muscadelle grape varieties.

An alternative choice if you want to go a little off-piste is to try a Viognier with a spicy starter. This is a rich and powerful white wine. If you want to go for the more expensive option then Condrieu is probably the best, but there are some fabulous examples all over the world, including the southern Rhône and Vin de Pays region of southern France. I would also recommend Riesling with a rich starter, but it does seem to be an acquired taste these days. Despite being better value, Riesling is generally ignored, as restaurants favour more popular grape varieties that imbibers feel more comfortable with.

The truth is you will sometimes find better value in grape varieties that are less well known. Pinot Grigio went through an incredibly popular period and the price went up dramatically on wines which in my opinion are about as interesting as Soave from Italy. I think it is another one of those inferior wines sold at an inflated price.

A popular white wine that I love to drink with starters, and which is often on wine lists, is Orvieto, from Umbria in Italy, which is one of the few decent Italian white wines. Make sure you choose a dry one, as there are many which are sweet.

One final option for a white wine that will complement a starter that I like is an Austrian Grüner Veltliner. It is spicy and full of fresh acidity, and goes tremendously well with shellfish. I can still remember a wonderful lunch at a Loch Fyne restaurant in Bath which started with fresh crab in its shell and a glass of "Grüner V" – simply delicious.

The mark-up on wine in a restaurant in the UK is notoriously astronomic; normally 300 to 400 per cent. So a ten-pound bottle in a wine shop is likely to be priced in a restaurant at around £30–40 per bottle. The restaurant will then suggest you leave a tip. I think a service charge should represent how satisfied you are as a client with the service, but in reality it is now a down payment for the service you will receive on your next visit to the restaurant.

You probably wouldn't want to follow in the footsteps of my Scottish grandfather, who, when he took my grandmother out to tea, would order a pot of tea for one and two cups. It was rumoured that he always carried two chequebooks with him – one which had no more cheques in the book, the other with plenty. If anyone demanded payment of a debt, he could produce an empty chequebook and apologise profusely to delay payment a little longer!

There was one occasion, when I was working behind the bar in a wine bar in London, when a fellow arrived who had been coming in virtually every day for months and always asked for the same bottle of red wine to share with his guest. I would ask him if he wanted his "usual" and he would normally answer in the affirmative. However, I remember one day he said, *"Yes, that will do nicely, but Graham, tomorrow I am coming in with my wife, and she mustn't know that I come here as often as I do, so please make sure you don't ask if I want my usual."* The following day, sure enough, he arrived with a lady and I pretended I had never met him. Having offered him the wine list, he chose a much less expensive wine than the one he usually selected. Now that's service!

There was another fellow who came into the bar every day and would ask me to tell him what sandwiches we had available for lunch. There was always a huge selection, and I would run through: egg, egg and cress, ham, ham and egg, cheese, cheese and pickle, cheese and tomato, rare roast beef, beef and horseradish, smoked salmon and cream cheese, etc., coming in total to about twenty different types. At the end, when I had gone through the lot, he would opt for the rare roast beef and horseradish. What's wrong with that, you might ask? Well nothing, except, having gone through all the options every day, he would choose the same sandwich each and every time. Often I'd say, *"Is it the usual, sir?"* but he would have none of it and insisted each time on me going through all the sandwiches on offer. There came a point when all the bar staff would pretend there were stairs behind the counter and disappear down below the level of the bar, out of sight, to avoid the gentleman in question, knowing full well what he would make us do.

Back to the wine list – I would recommend avoiding house wines, as in my experience they will be less good value than other wines on the list. Often these wines are of inferior quality with an even bigger margin added. The reason for this is many people who do not know anything about wine just ask for a bottle of the house white or red. These are the volume wines for many restaurants, on which they will load a margin.

Sometimes restaurants will have a special wine of the month, which could well be better value, as a merchant may have offered a special discount at a better margin to try and encourage the restaurant to take a new line and it may have a greater volume to sell. It's worth asking the wine waiter if it's any good; he may even let you taste a little before ordering.

Occasionally, in a more informal setting, it is worth ordering some glasses of wine at the beginning to see what you like and then ordering bottles of the samples you like best.

Choose grape varieties you feel comfortable with from the New World. There is a consistency and a simplicity with the wines from the Southern Hemisphere, since most of the wines are named after their grape variety. The only danger with New World wines is their level of alcohol, which, depending on whether it is lunch or dinner, should be considered. At lunch, lighter, less alcoholic wines are generally more popular. New World wines are beginning to rise in alcohol as a result of warmer weather in the vineyards.

A good-value consistent red wine which goes with any red meat is Rioja from Spain. Navarra, a neighbouring wine region, is less well known and better value. Châteauneuf-du-Pape is probably the most popular wine ordered in restaurants in the UK, because for some reason everyone has heard of it. It is consequently sold in huge quantities and often is poor quality, as the vineyards are able to trade on their name. Check the vintage too, as these tend to be very youthful and really far too young to drink. There was one person who had just ordered Châteauneuf-du-Pape in a restaurant, and when the wine waiter asked discreetly why he had ordered this wine he replied, *"Well, it sounds so good!"*

Much better would be to buy a bottle of Gigondas, which is a neighbouring village to Châteauneuf in the southern Rhône Valley, but less well known and consequently better value. Another village which is not well known and terrific value is Sablet, but Vacqueyras and Carpentras are also better-value reds from the southern Rhône, almost as good as a Châteauneuf, but much less expensive.

Shiraz from Australia, Cabernet from California, Merlot from Chile, Sauvignon or Pinot Noir from New Zealand will all be a safe choice too. For red wines you generally want to choose older vintages which will be drinking better and be more mature. Drinking a bottle of very young fine red wine can often be an unpleasant experience, as the harsh tannins pucker the mouth and the taste will be like fruit juice, rather than with more appealing, softer, complex characters. Approaching a fine red wine too early is just infanticide. By taking a little more time and waiting, patience will be rewarded. Choose younger white wines, as these wines display intensity, vitality and freshness in their youth.

Occasionally, and it is more seldom than it used to be – when the wine waiter gives you a small tasting of your selected wine – the wine will smell of wet socks, wet sacks, a sort of musty and rather unpleasant aroma of damp dog. This indicates that the wine is corked, although increasingly restaurants are serving wines with screw tops, so there is no chance at all of this being the fault. Sometimes corkiness can't be detected on the nose, so it is important to taste the wine as well as smelling it before you accept it. The taste of corkiness is a foul, mean and musty flavour, where the fruit has been completely subdued. Technically it is called trichloroanisole or TCA, which is a chlorine by-product used to sterilise corks, but which is sometimes not entirely removed and results in cork taint.

Oxidised wine can be a problem too: here the wine has aged prematurely in bottle because too much air has entered the bottle through a faulty cork. The wine will smell of sherry and have changed colour to a brown tawny hue for reds and a deeper yellowy orange colour for whites.

Since restaurant-goers are paying such a high mark-up on each bottle consumed, it is worth sending a wine back if you detect corkiness or some other fault. About one in ten bottles has been found to be faulty in a restaurant, exacerbated by the fact that often wines are not stored appropriately – on their side in a constant cool temperature. Politely saying *"This wine is off, please bring me another bottle"* is the simplest and most direct recommended statement. I would advise against *"um, I think there may be something wrong with the wine"*. By all means ask the wine waiter to taste it for confirmation.

I prefer lighter wines at lunch, so generally choose white wines and red grapes such a Pinot Noir and Gamay in the summer. Wines from the Loire Valley in France tend to be a little lighter than wines further south, particularly the Cabernet Franc. I think red Rhône wines generally tend to be better value than clarets, so when I am dining in a restaurant I tend to opt for them. They also go best with any sort of game, which I don't tend to eat at home as often as in restaurants.

Pinot Noir is a versatile grape variety to choose in a restaurant. For cooked fish I would recommend a New World Pinot Noir from the cooler climates of New Zealand, Australia, Oregon and Carneros in California. New World Pinot Noirs tend to be a little softer and juicier, with a balanced acidity which will blend beautifully with the texture of most fish. Rich cheesy or white sauces will also go really well with this red grape variety. As it is one of my favourite grape varieties, I also prefer to drink Pinot Noir with lighter meats such as chicken and pork, and it is particularly delicious with roast duck. Since duck is richer, I would probably choose a red Burgundy rather than a New World Pinot, as the tannins will complement the fattiness of the meat.

For stews and richer, gamey dishes, I would recommend the Syrah grape variety in a restaurant. Either New World or the northern Rhône Valley, but if you choose the Rhône, again the older vintages of Saint-Joseph, Crozes-Hermitage, Hermitage, Cornas and Côte-Rôtie should be better value than an older vintage from a classified growth in Bordeaux. In fact, an older but dependable vintage from a good year of Vacqueyras or Sablet would be decent value.

For darker meats such as lamb and beef, I would recommend Claret, Rioja or Argentinean Cabernet or Malbec. The texture of the meat will be enhanced by the stronger tannins and power of these wines.

Finally, if you have time, and I would make time for a special occasion, I would suggest a glass of sweet wine to go with your pudding. Most decent restaurants will offer sweet wine by the glass, and I would recommend Muscat de Beaumes-de-Venise (for me the best is the Domaine de Durban), Sauternes or Tokay, depending on your wallet and what is available. My favourite early drinking sweet white wine is Cyprès de Climens from Barsac, the second wine of the famous Château.

As Jancis Robinson wrote:

"Every glass of wine we drink represents a whole year of vineyard cultivation and perhaps several years of effort in the winery… Yet most of us throw it away, straight down our throats, without even trying to 'read' it."

When visiting a restaurant, it is so enjoyable to relax, take your time and savour the moments of being looked after and waited upon in good company. The most important thing is not to be intimidated by anyone and make your wine selection confidently.

As Derek Cooper wrote in *Wine with Food*:

"As long as we remember the distinctions that ought to be drawn between what we like and what we think we ought to like, then we'll preserve our sense of proportion and humour. Wine is there, like food, to be enjoyed; an occasion for relaxation. If we're going to worry about it then we'd be better off putting the corkscrew back in the drawer."

So if I had to choose one restaurant in the UK, which would it be? As you know, when I am buying wine in a restaurant I like to go for the best value and quality combined, generally not the well-known brands, quite often a wine from a good year which is reliable and often off the beaten track. So the best lunch I have ever had was at the Hind's Head pub in Bray, which is owned by Heston Blumenthal, but is nothing like as expensive as the better-known Fat Duck in the same village. Here the food is simply delicious. I had the finest warm scotch egg I have ever tasted – simple cooking, not overly expensive but of an incredibly high standard.

Worth every penny!

"Wine is one of the most civilised things in the world and one of the natural things of the world that has been brought to the greatest perfection, and it offers a greater range for enjoyment and appreciation than, possibly, any other purely sensory thing which may be purchased."
Ernest Hemingway, from *Death in the Afternoon* (1932)

Exploring the wines of Argentina is a thrilling experience; their intense fruit flavours seductively dance the tango on your tongue. Malbec is synonymous with Mendoza, but there is so much more in this exciting vineyard area, which deserves greater recognition on the world wine stage. Ideally a glass of Malbec should be accompanied by a flame-grilled cut of grass-fed, free-range beef from the Pampas.

It's not only the wine and the meat that is exciting in Argentina. On my first visit, I wasn't sure whether to drive myself around Mendoza, as I usually do in a vineyard region, or to hire a driver. It didn't take long to realise that I definitely needed to get a local to drive me around the vineyards. The driving conditions in Mendoza are extremely hazardous, with red lights appearing to indicate an optional stop and road signs being either cleverly concealed or non-existent. I was also a little concerned to read in the newspapers that a man had been shot for his shoes a couple of weeks before I arrived. My flip-flops were used rather more during this visit than I had originally intended.

It was while travelling in my chauffeured car, whilst considering whether parental consumption of wine tends to sire girls rather than boys (there seem to be five women for each man in Argentina), that I was suddenly startled by the noise of the terrifying soundtrack in that scary film *Psycho* – picture the shadow of the dagger on the shower curtain. It was coming from my driver's mobile phone. I suggested to Miguel that he could have chosen a more melodious ringtone, but he replied that he had programmed this tune especially and exclusively for when his ex-wife called. Later on, I was interrupted again from working out what little profit is left on a bottle of wine once you've shipped it, paid tax, stored and delivered it to a client, when I was interrupted again, but this time by a rather lovely melody emanating from my driver's mobile phone. *"That's a much better ringtone,"* I suggested. *"Yes, this one is for my latest girlfriend!"* said Miguel as he guffawed with laughter.

The key influence on the wines produced in the Mendoza wine region is its altitude. Some vineyards are 2,000 metres above sea level. The cold nights and dry sunny days combine to concentrate the flavours and enhance the aromatics in these wonderfully ripe, fruity wines. The diurnal variation gives heat during the summer of up to 40 degrees during the day, falling at night-time to 12 degrees. The effect is to lengthen the growing season, so that the grapes ripen more gradually over a longer period, giving rise to more characterful, complex and flavoursome wines. It is during the cool nights that the vines manage to sleep, whereas in a hot climate with warm nights the vines never get that chance, ripening as they do in a much shorter season.

The quality of the wines is a direct consequence of the gradual, slow-growing season. To prolong it even further for white wines, the vines are planted east to west, letting the vines receive more protection from the sun. For the warmer red-wine-producing vines such as the Malbec, Syrah and Cabernet, the vines are planted in north-south rows, giving less shadow and allowing the ripening berries more sunshine.

Mendoza would be a desert, with only 200 millimetres of rain falling per year, were it not for an elaborate network of trenches, first developed by the indigenous Huarpe people, which cool the city and irrigate the surrounding vineyards and are supplied by the snow melt, which is efficiently collected and redirected. Mendoza itself would be stiflingly hot if it weren't for the extensive plantings of plane trees throughout the city. The wind, known as the Zonda, never ceases, and it keeps the vines cool in the very hot sunshine.

The melted snow from the Andes mountains is used to irrigate the vines and this gives the wine a purity and minerality which is quite exceptional.

The best vineyards in Argentina use a precise drip-irrigation system, so that each of the vines receives exactly the right amount of water to maintain the balance and concentration in the grapes during the hotter spells in midsummer. A black hose passes along the row of vines, with a hole above each vine, through which small, carefully calibrated quantities of water can be spilled only when required. Foxes have become a slight problem for some vineyards, as the animals chew through the hose in the knowledge of a plentiful supply of fresh water inside.

In Chile, the local streams are sometimes redirected, creating a small lake across the vineyard as the vines drink voraciously during the heat of the summer. This is known as flood irrigation. Sometimes the vines will take in too much water, causing the grapes to swell, and potentially diluting the grape juice.

As I fly from cloudy Santiago over the snow-capped peaks, peering up through the clouds, suddenly the vista opens up and the clouds disappear, revealing the Argentinean Andes range and the vineyards stretched out along the foothills, bathed in sunshine. Their wines are truly bottled sunshine with a sonnet of poetry thrown in beneath the cork. Here some of the wines are terrific value and fine quality. I think Argentina is the most exciting wine region in the world right now.

Just before the turn of the 21st century, Argentina stopped producing oxidised alcoholic plonk and started to concentrate on quality for the export market. This was mainly from commercial necessity, since the domestic consumption of wine has dropped from 92 litres per head in 1970 to 35 litres in 2000. No more flood irrigation, no more warm fermentation, no more throwing in every grape possible into the vat to create the maximum volume. Now with a plentiful supply of inexpensive labour, Argentina can produce stunning wines at a reasonable cost.

It is no wonder that Chilean wineries, French *négociants*, wealthy Americans and Dutch entrepreneurs are investing in this region; a region which has been achieving a 33% growth in exports each year.

The 2002 currency devaluation of the peso, escaping the peg of the dollar, has made exporting much easier and made Argentinean wines much better value for money.

Because the winters are cold and the summers are dry and hot, there is very little disease. Whilst the pale-yellow sap-sucking phylloxera insect destroyed the vineyards of Europe during the late 19th century, it has not so far dared to infest the vines of Argentina. A further bonus for the vine growers is that there is little need for pesticides and chemical spraying in this healthy, disease-free environment, so that the wines can be said to be more natural.

The top grape, or the most widely grown here, is the renowned Malbec. It was once widely grown in Bordeaux and is the main constituent of the dense tannic rustic wines of Cahors, and it enjoyed great popularity in Russia during the reign of Peter the Great. At six foot eight in height, Peter probably needed a big powerful wine to satisfy his thirst, and Malbec is just the thing for that. It was during the 19th century that the grape made its way to Mendoza, which is about 600 miles west of Buenos Aires, across the sweeping grasslands of the Pampas.

Argentina is not the sort of place I would encourage a vegetarian to explore. The perfect accompaniment for these spicy, rich and fruity Malbec wines is beef – but beef like no other you have tasted: this is fresh, grass-fed, leaner meat, gamier, chewier and more flavoursome than anything I have tasted in Europe. If you go to Mendoza, try the Don Mario restaurant, which I reckon serves the best flame-grilled meat in Mendoza. It is a humble, unassuming restaurant, located slightly off the beaten track in a back street. There are bars across the windows nearby, but the cuts of meat are absolutely magnificent. This is carnivore heaven.

There is a delicious thrill of discovery for a wine explorer like me as you swirl the Malbec around your mouth, the texture of the beef and the tannins in the wine blending together in the most sumptuous fusion.

As any gaucho will tell you, Argentina is not a one-trick pony. Mendoza is not just about Malbec. The cooler and higher sites are producing some top-notch Chardonnay, which, with judicious use of French oak, taste surprisingly similar to top-quality white Burgundy. The Torrontés grape is producing some of the most powerfully aromatic white wine I have ever tasted, which is certainly worth considering as an aperitif. Merlot is also performing well, giving an intensity of fruit flavour, coupled with a silkiness in which Saint-Émilion lovers will delight. Both Cabernet Sauvignon and Syrah grapes are producing some impressive wines, even from some of the younger vines. The potential here, in my view, is greater than in the more well-known, more developed vineyards of Chile. Even Pinot Noir is now being planted further north in Salta and further south in Patagonia, in some of the higher, cooler vineyard sites. I believe this difficult beast has an interesting future in Argentina once the vines have more age.

However, I still think that if you are looking for white wines from a South American cool climate that are not too alcoholic, there is a small region just north of Santiago in Chile called Casablanca, and it is here that you will find the most delicious Sauvignon Blanc wines from South America. Again, these wines are probably slightly better value than the Sauvignons coming from New Zealand.

My favourite vineyard in Argentina is the Tempus Alba vineyard in Maipu in Mendoza. If you fly into Mendoza, it is only a short drive from the city. This was a fabulous discovery; the name literally means "Time of the Dawn", which is the time when the vineyards are harvested. To preserve the primary fruit aromas and encourage focus in the wines, picking the grapes in the cool of the dawn means you don't allow the grapes to oxidise in the heat of the daily sunshine.

I turned up at this winery after Miguel my driver suggested that this was a vineyard worth visiting. I had vaguely heard of it, so I thought I would give it a try.

I was met by Sibila Genolet, a charming Argentinean lady who helps runs the vineyard with her Italian husband and is also the fourth generation in her family to toil in the wine industry. There is something in the Argentinean psyche that is incredibly welcoming and warm-hearted. Sibila was no exception, and I was made to feel very much at home.

I tasted through their entire selection of wines sitting on the roof terrace of the winery, surrounded by their vineyards and trying not to be distracted by the view of the snow-capped peaks in the distance. These Tempus wines are so good they are even exported to France. Some of the vines are over sixty years old, located high up in the Andes foothills at 1,200 metres above sea level. The age of the vines, as you know by now, gives the wine added finesse, complexity and depth.

These really are outstandingly fine wines and represent good value for money. I only import their red wines – I don't touch the whites and their rosé, known as rosso, which is too alcoholic and dark red for my liking, although in the heat of the summer sunshine in Argentina I'm sure these wines are popular.

Tempus have been working for twenty years on identifying the perfect clone of Malbec, and finally now produce a Malbec called Vero, which they consider to be that clone. It is the most sublime wine.

If you decide to visit Mendoza I would recommend staying at the Park Hyatt Hotel, close to Independence Square. It's not cheap, but it is a delightful place to take cover after a hard day tasting and talking. In Mendoza the vintage takes place generally at the end of February, so I'd recommend visiting in January, when the vineyards look beautiful in the warm sunshine and the weather in the Northern Hemisphere is often so cold, bleak and grey.

As a contrast to downtown Mendoza, I would recommend staying upcountry in the Uco Valley at the Posada Salentein. It is a very special place, surrounded by its own excellent vineyards producing some delightful wines. The Posada is nestled in the middle of vineyards, where a soul can roam after a decent bibulous supper in the gathering evening twilight and reflect on life's opportunities and challenges.

My visit to the Valle de Uco was finished off with an early-morning horse ride with a gaucho named Jesus, who took me galloping through apple orchards, olive groves and long pampas grass close to the vineyards, beside fierce rushing streams in the shadow of the snow-capped peaks of the magnificent Andes mountains. It was a memorable experience – my trip with Jesus!

The red wines of Argentina have a delicious concentration to them which is almost unique. The wines could be characterised as an iron hand in a velvet glove. They combine power and silkiness, intensity and richness, which for my palate is a joy to taste. The alcohol levels are high, but they are perfectly in balance: the alcohol doesn't dominate the wine because the fruit is so powerful too. These wines are designed to be enjoyed with food, and most obviously a steak. My preference is for rib steak, which I believe has more flavour than fillet, rump or sirloin. Equally, you could enjoy these special red wines with lamb, venison, wilder dark meats or a rich stew. My only advice is don't drive afterwards – make sure you have a driver.

Drinking and driving is a serious mistake. As you well know, some have been known to have brushes with the authorities on their way home from the odd social occasion over the years. One particular driver decided to do something about it. One night he was out for a few drinks with some friends and had a few too many glasses of Torrontés, as well as Chardonnay, washed down by some rather nice Malbec; but knowing full well he may have been slightly over the limit, he did something he'd never done before – he took a bus home. He arrived back safely and without incident, which was a real surprise, since he had never driven one before!

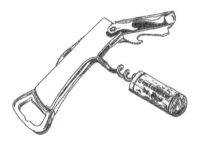

"Wine-drinking is no occult art to be practised only by the gifted few. It is, or should be, the sober habit of every normal man or woman burdened with normal responsibilities and with a normal desire to keep their problems in perspective and themselves in good health."
Allan Sichel (1900–1965)

It was Allan Sichel's son Peter who first introduced me to the real magic of wine. I stayed in Bordeaux for about a month to learn about vinous matters whilst working for the renowned Sichel *négociant* in their office on the Quai de Bacalan on the banks of the great river Garonne.

Each night, Peter would put his head around my door and enquire, *"So, Graham, what have you learnt today?"* Each night I would try and come up with some intelligent nugget that would impress my mentor. Actually, the truth, beyond understanding the technical and intellectual aspects of wine, which I didn't learn until much later, is it comes down in the end to what *excites* you. The good news is that wine is not only thrilling but it's beneficial to one's health if prescribed in sensible, moderate quantities.

"I once woke up in a drawer at the bottom of a wardrobe. That was fairly frightening. Try opening a drawer from the inside. It's quite tricky."
Jeffrey Bernard

The definition of an alcoholic is, I am told, someone who drinks more than his doctor. A friend of mine went to see his doctor and was asked how much he drank. He replied that he imbibed about a bottle of wine a day on average. The doctor admitted that he normally doubled the amount of alcohol a patient declared, so he would be noting a total of two bottles per day as his considered, more realistic consumption.

As my friend was leaving the surgery he asked the doctor what would be a sensible healthy amount to drink each day. The doctor replied for a man it is three units per day. *"But that's nearly a bottle a day."*

"No it isn't: it is more like half a bottle a day," said the doctor.

"Ah yes," my friend responded, *"but you doubled my assessment on the way in, so I'm doubling your analysis on the way out!"*

Curiously, there are an enormous number of doctors who have joined the wine industry – over 300 in Australia have set up their own vineyards. Is it just a coincidence? There are certainly plenty of proverbs and sayings that indicate that wine is a healthy drink.

"He who drinks a glass of wine a day will live to die another way."
Latin Proverb

"A tax on wine is a tax on the health of our citizens!"
Thomas Jefferson (1743–1826)

"Drink a glass of wine with your soup and steal a ruble from your doctor."
Russian Proverb

"Grapes from whence strong drink is derived is healing for mankind."
The Koran

There is no doubt that drinking too much clearly damages health, and probably drinking too little doesn't improve health, so what is the right amount of wine to prescribe?

AIM – Alcohol in Moderation – was founded in 1991 as an independent organisation whose role is to communicate "The Responsible Drinking Message", and to act as a conduit for information from the industry, its associations and relevant medical and scientific researchers, legislation, policy and campaigns. Alcohol in Moderation stipulates that in the UK levels of alcohol consumption unlikely to cause health damage *"are defined as 3 to 4 units (8g) per day for men, and 2 to 3 units per day for women".* The UK message is unique in that it also gives a guideline or limit for weekly consumption, which is 21 units for men and 14 units per week for women. A unit is about a small glass of wine. AIM goes on to say, *"In addition, a maximum health advantage of between one and two daily units is noted, and it is emphasised that a significant health risk will not accrue up to four units a day for men and three units a day for women."* The guidelines also discuss that *"the health benefits are more evident from regular daily drinking".* Specifically, men over the age of 40 and post-menopausal women are emphasised as recipients of a *"significant health benefit in terms of reduced coronary heart disease mortality and morbidity"*. Furthermore, the guidelines explain that middle-aged or elderly non-drinkers or infrequent drinkers and especially those at risk from heart disease *"may wish to consider the possibility that light drinking may be of benefit to their overall health and life expectancy"*.

It was the French paradox which started it all off. How come the French could eat such an appalling diet of fatty foods drenched in rich oily sauces whilst at the same time living longer than us Brits? The oldest lady in the world up until a few years ago lived in Champagne until she was 125. A journalist from *The Evening Standard* went out to interview her and offered to get her a glass of water. *"Mon Dieu, water is for frogs, get me a glass of champagne,"* she retorted. Perhaps the truth does come out in wine, *in vino veritas*, as it leads those of an enquiring mind to discover that regular moderate drinking of red wine has serious significant health benefits.

Dr Thomas Stuttaford, who used to write regularly for the *Times* published a book: *To Your Good Health! The Wise Drinker's Guide* (Faber & Faber), which rather challenged medical orthodoxy with good-humoured advice to sensible drinkers. The benefits of alcohol in terms of heart disease are well known, but other *benefits* are less well publicised. According to the evidence that Dr Stuttaford produces, moderate alcohol consumption lowers the risk of late-onset diabetes, helps prevents strokes and improves the sperm count. The intellect is even sharpened, especially in older people, and the onset of Alzheimer's is reduced.

There is a host of scientific research which supports this view.

In the UK we are even prescribing red wine on the National Health Service for heart patients. The reason is that red wine contains a compound called resveratrol, which is found in the red grape skin. This compound has the effect of thinning the blood, breaking down bad cholesterol and widening the arteries. The effect is to reduce the pressure on the heart to pump blood around the body, as the thinner blood circulates more easily through wider more cavernous arteries.

Maurice, an eighty-year-old man, went to see his doctor with a heart complaint. The doctor was horrified to see Maurice skipping down the road a couple of days later with a very young, energetic, fit-looking blonde on his arm. Maurice bounded up to his doctor and declared, "Just doing what you said, doc – get a hot mumma and be cheerful."

The doctor replied, "I didn't say that: I said you've got a heart murmur; be careful."

Historically people used to drink a lot more than they do today. It is not an accident that a standard bottle of wine is 75 centilitres of liquid. This was the volume of wine that it was considered a French artisan could drink satisfactorily with his meal at one sitting. It is probably not a coincidence that in olden days people didn't live as long as they do today. I've also noticed in France and southern European nations that a good two hours is taken at lunchtime, so as to enable them to return to afternoon work refreshed. Perhaps this too has something to do with their longevity when compared to the British "sandwich at the desk" lunch mentality. Surely it is the quality of life rather than the length of life which is most important?

As Oscar Wilde wrote, *"Only dull people are brilliant at breakfast,"* and as Phil Harris said, *"I feel sorry for people who don't drink. When they wake up in the morning, that's as good as they're going to feel all day"*. Whereas for the rest of us who enjoy a glass or two, the day can just get better and better and better!

Hangovers are mainly caused by dehydration. After drinking perhaps rather more than modestly, the brain swells so that it no longer fits snugly inside your cranium, but is compressed hard up against the inside of your skull, and this pressure causes the headache.

One of the advantages of getting older is that when you get to my age your brain has shrunk so much that there is room for it to expand after drinking.

I was once told that you can only drink too fast and not too much, and perhaps there is some truth in this. Take it slowly.

"Whether wine is a nourishment, medicine or poison is a matter of dosage." Paracelsus (1493–1541), father of modern pharmacology.

There is a true story of Lady Astor, the first female MP, who used to entertain the Cabinet of the day at her famous house Cliveden, in Berkshire, before it became a hotel. One evening she was sitting down to dinner when she noticed that the wine waiter was drunk. She discreetly called him over and placed a handwritten note on his tray which read, "You're drunk – leave the room immediately." She was then horrified to see the wine waiter stagger in a slightly haphazard manner around the table to where the Foreign Secretary was sitting and, rather ostentatiously, placed the note down directly in front of him.

Not only is wine considered beneficial for health, but it has now been proved that there is a correlation between wine consumption and

IQ. No, it is not the simple relationship you would at first think. The Americans carried out an analysis to see whether there was a connection between IQ and wine consumption in three groups of over-sixties. The three groups were those who had never drunk any form of alcohol at all, those who drank 2–3 glasses of wine per day and those who drank a bottle a day or more (that they could find who were still alive). Their findings were interesting. Those who drank 2–3 glasses of wine a day had a higher IQ than those who drank nothing at all. Unfortunately those who drank a bottle a day had a lower IQ than those who were teetotal. The message is, therefore, that moderation is not just for monks, and great minds drink alike!

But are there any lessons to be learnt from the wine world in terms of promoting personal happiness?

It was Benjamin Franklin who said, *"Wine is constant proof that God loves us and wants us to be happy,"* and even Sir Alexander Fleming said, *"Penicillin cures but wine makes us happy."*

There is the old story of a professor who was giving a lecture on the relationship between the frequency of making love and happiness. He argued that the higher the frequency of making love, the happier the person would be. So for the climax of his speech he asked all those in the audience who made love at least once a day to put their hands up, and they all looked really happy. He then asked all those who made love once a week to put their hands up, and they looked quite happy, but not as happy as the first selection. He then asked all those who made love once a month to put up their hands and they looked decidedly grumpy and sad. Finally, to confirm his thesis, he asked all those who made love once a year to raise their hands, and a little old man right at the back of the hall raised his hand, looking very, very happy indeed. This was a concern for the professor, because this evidence didn't tie in with his findings at all. *"Why are you looking so happy?"* he asked the old man.

"It's tonight, it's tonight!"

I think this theory of happiness can also be used for the frequency of having the pleasure of sharing a fine bottle of wine with good friends.

It is about time the Nanny State acknowledged that life is not just about quantity – how long you live – but quality – how many good times and how many good bottles you have along the way. We have all witnessed real joy, happiness and pleasure amongst friends enjoying much laughter and camaraderie, which is the wondrous alchemy of a bottle of wine shared, whatever the price.

So, here's to your good health and happiness!

"When God made the world there was one country that was filled with the most magnificent mountains, immensely fertile soil and immeasurably beautiful lakes. So to compensate the rest of the world for this, He populated this country with French people and called the country France." Anon.

I have dabbled with so many wonderful wines from the New World, but I always finally return to France for the very finest and most expensive wines. I appreciate the beautifully balanced Chardonnays from Marlborough in New Zealand, the powerful Chardonnays from Carneros in California, the rich Chardonnays from the Yarra Valley and the delicious Chardonnays from Margaret River in Australia. But, if you want the finest, you have to explore Burgundy, where it all started. One must pay a premium for the best, but if you want the most classy, elegant fine wines crafted from the Chardonnay grape, I think you have to return to the Côte de Beaune, the gorgeous vineyards of Burgundy, and sample Corton-Charlemagne, Meursault, Puligny-Montrachet and Chassagne-Montrachet from the finest years.

Here in the Côte d'Or, the golden hillside which faces south-east, the vines receive the gentle morning sunshine which ripens the grapes slowly and produces the depth and character that all lovers of fine wine cherish.

No one is absolutely sure why it is known as the Côte d'Or; some believe it is because of the golden colour the vine leaves turn in the autumn just before they fall to the ground. Others believe it is because these ancient east-facing hills face the Orient. Those of us in the wine trade, however, believe it's called the "golden hill" because the wines are so flaming expensive.

If you want to taste the finest, most complete Sauvignons in the world, there will be a discussion about including the explosive, fruit-driven wines from Marlborough in New Zealand, Tasmania in Australia or Casablanca in Chile, but ultimately, in my view, you have to head for the Loire Valley in France and to Pouilly-Fumé and Sancerre. The best of these wines have the intensity of fruit character from the New World coupled with a minerality, elegance and finesse that it is difficult to find outside France. But you will have to pay top dollar for the finest of these wines; one such is the Baron de L from Château du Nozet in Pouilly-sur-Loire. This is probably the finest expression of Sauvignon Blanc that I have discovered. It has a vibrant, golden-green colour, and on the nose it is a harmonious blend of strength and freshness with orange peel, grapefruit, beeswax and floral hints. On the palate the fruit is full and elegant, showing a mineral complexity combined with herbaceous fruit and zesty acidity. The length of the wine on the finish is extraordinary. Unlike most other Sauvignon Blancs it has the potential to age for 5–10 years and more.

If you are searching for the finest "fizz", you will probably end up in Champagne, drinking vintage Krug or Roederer Cristal. Vintage champagne is made in the year in which the grapes have been produced, whereas a non-vintage is made from grapes grown from a collection of years blended to a brand flavour profile which will display consistency from year to year. Vintage champagne is much more expensive than non-vintage. Incidentally, the UK is producing some of the finest vintage sparkling wines in the world, which are not allowed to be called champagne but are nonetheless outstandingly good. I'm thinking, of course, of Nyetimber, which is served at Buckingham Palace and Downing Street, particularly when there is a French President to entertain! In my experience one never regrets one's extravagances...

Champagne is made traditionally from three grape varieties (two being red) in differing proportions, Pinot Noir, Pinot Meunier and Chardonnay. The real work goes on in the cellar as the fizz is created from a second fermentation which is created in the bottle. A dry white wine has a little yeast and sugar added to it to start the second fermentation. The yeast starts gobbling up the sugar and then produce alcohol and carbon dioxide as a by-product. A crown capsule seals the bottle, so that the carbon dioxide emanating from the second fermentation cannot escape, and hence the fizz in champagne is generated entirely from the second fermentation inside the actual bottle you have bought. The dead yeast cells fall to the bottom of the bottle. The bottles are gradually turned upside down during this process, called *riddling*, so the yeast gunk collects in the neck of the bottle, sitting on top of the crown cap with the bottle held upside down. The neck of the bottle is then passed through freezing brine so that the gunk becomes ice, the crown cap is then taken off, the ice pops out from the built-up pressure in the bottle and a small amount of champagne is added to top up the bottle, and a wired cork is then used as the seal. The liquid inside is now perfectly clear champagne.

The glass used to make champagne bottles is heavier, thicker and more robust than that used on normal wine bottles, because of the increased pressure inside the bottle. This pressure is about the same as the pressure in the enormous tyres of the London Routemaster bus.

I once attended a seminar on champagne where the lecturer took a bottle of champagne and attempted to demonstrate the best way to open it. He said, *"You need to turn the bottle onto a 45-degree angle and gently ease the cork out little by little, so that it makes the sound of the sigh of a contented lady."* At which point there was an enormous bang, as the cork shot off into the air and hit the ceiling. There was an Australian winemaker sitting on my right who, to roars of laughter, shouted out, *"I know her!"*

The cheapest and most exciting bottle of sparkling wine I have ever tasted was sitting astride the Berlin Wall with some friends well before it came down, and firing the cork towards East German territory. I raised a glass and toasted freedom as I watched the East German machine-gun barrels turn towards me and my comrades. I then climbed down off the wall incredibly quickly. My only recommendation when drinking champagne is to drink it slowly and enjoy every sip – don't rush it like you're about to be shot.

As Graham Harding writes in *A Wine Miscellany*:

"The smaller the bubble, the better the champagne. Large bubbles are the mark of lesser sparklers and are dismissed by the French as oeils de crapaud or "toads' eyes"... The average bottle of champagne contains about 49 million bubbles... When the bubble reaches the surface of the glass it ruptures and a tiny jet of wine is released, which reaches several centimetres above the surface – the tickle effect."

Krug is probably the finest vintage champagne. Fermented in oak, it is given an extra richness and depth which balances exquisitely with fruit intensity. The only major consideration regarding drinking a bottle of Krug is: *"If I share this with someone else, will they enjoy it as much as I will?"*

Bollinger vintage is another favourite of mine; it is fermented in oak *barriques*, and is the driest of the great vintages.

Louis Roederer is the most successful of the smaller great champagne houses. The *cuvée* includes sufficient Chardonnay to give it a refined, creamy-biscuity complexity, which is usually apparent in its non-vintage Brut Premier, but in the vintage *cuvée* this can take two or three years to evolve. Louis Roederer was founded in 1776. In 1876, Louis Roederer II, who had succeeded his father, created the Cristal *cuvée* for Tsar Alexander II. In 1909, Tsar Nicolas II nominated Louis Roederer as the official supplier to the Imperial Court of Russia. Cristal has more depth and intensity, but also a delightful power and richness balanced with firm acidity and a delightful hint of brioche. It does need to be kept for a few years before it tells the whole story. The Roederer vintage is another Pinot Noir-dominated champagne, combined with 34% Chardonnay. I was exploring Rheims recently and was lucky enough to taste this champagne; it has poise, elegance and balance, and for a vintage wine is reasonable value.

Veuve Clicquot was the first house to devise a system to draw out the sediment, called *remuage*. Clicquot is more full-bodied, boasting tremendous elegance and toasty complexity. In my experience it flows rather well at Lord's Cricket Ground.

Pol Roger was Churchill's favourite champagne. It was Churchill who said of champagne: *"In victory we deserve it, in defeat we need it."* At the launch of the Cuvée Sir Winston Churchill in 1984, Lady Soames said of her father's passion for Pol Roger: *"I saw him many times the better for it, but never the worse."* Pol Roger's fragrant, creamy, lemony, non-vintage style tends to last longer and remain fresher than those of any other house.

Pommery, on the other hand, is much lighter, singing the higher notes to me, but perfumed and vivacious.

Ruinart is the oldest house, founded in 1729; the non-vintage has an attractive minerally flavour, great finesse and represents good value.

But for me the best-value quality champagne is the less well-known J-P Robert Cuvée Reserve champagne, which is an old favourite of mine.

J-P Robert is 80% Pinot Noir, and it is a truth universally acknowledged that the best champagnes tend to have a high proportion of Pinot Noir, which gives the wine its backbone and distinction. It comes from a small family-owned producer in the Aube, and I call it poor man's Krug because it has many of the characteristics of Krug: it is a rich, toasty and creamy champagne, with a honeyed depth balanced with a tingling fine finish. It is so much better than the sub-£20 champagnes, which tend to be lean, mean and often viciously acidic. At just over £20 a bottle, this is tremendous value.

I present a number of tutored wine tastings each year, when the labels are concealed in a blind tasting to see what really counts – the taste of the liquid inside the bottle rather than the label.

I showed Krug non-vintage against J-P Robert NV, and over half the punters preferred J-P Robert. This was telling, since you could have five bottles of the J-P for the same price as a single bottle of Krug. That is the heart of my job: to secure wines which are top value.

I remember a few years ago during a test match at Lord's, I donated a bottle of J-P Robert to the *Test Match Special* team, and I can confirm that the commentary improved, despite all the references to cakes and pigeons.

In France historically the individual vintage has been very important, because the weather can vary widely from year to year. For example, the 1992 vintage in Bordeaux was tragic because it rained before, during and after the vintage. The wines were diluted and lacked concentration and character. The 1990 vintage, or the 2003, 2009 and 2010 years, on the other hand, were fabulous. There was warm, sunny weather right up to and through the vintage, and the grapes were picked in perfect condition. If you buy any wine from Bordeaux in those years it will be superbly balanced. Virtually all the wines in 1992, 1993, 2002, 2011 and 2012, on the other hand, were, as the French like to say, "average".

The vintages in the cooler climates of the world such as Germany, where the vines just about manage to ripen the grapes, will have greater variation than those in warmer climates. I would argue that these climates will produce the best wines in the world in the good years, but in the bad years will be worse than the more temperate and consistent climates of the New World vineyards. The climates of the New World are more consistent from year to year, and therefore the vintages are less variable and can be purchased more confidently without having to know which year was a good, or less good, vintage.

In France, because of the marginal climate and variable weather, choosing which vintage to buy is therefore of crucial importance. I remember visiting a vineyard in the Rhône Valley in 2003, where I knew the weather had been poor during the previous vintage. Many of the vineyards picked the grapes after the rain, so the wines were diluted, thin, pale and lacking concentration. The winemaker told me that he had cleverly managed to pick the grapes before the rain, so his wines were rather better than those of his neighbours. When he poured out the wine, it was pink, almost like rosé, and I immediately knew his wines were also affected by the poor weather. I have never bought from this vineyard since this encounter!

The Rhône has tended to be better value than Bordeaux in the past. In the northern Rhône Valley, near the villages of Tain and Tournon, is the grand hill of Hermitage.

This hill looks like a replica of the hill in Hollywood, where the huge signs advertising the great *négociants* of Chapoutier and Jaboulet impose themselves in a similar way. Looking down from on high, through the steep rows of fine old vines you will discover where the greatest Syrahs of all time have been sired for over two thousand years. Forget Barossa and Penfolds, forget McLaren Vale Shiraz, forget all the rich, ripe, fruit-driven simple Shiraz from Stellenbosch, Mendoza and California, where so often the alcohol envelops the wine in its tight embrace. It is in the northern Rhône valley of France where the finest and most complex expression of the Syrah grape, in my view, is crafted, but only in the best years.

The hill of Hermitage took its name from one of the Knights Templar who, on his way home after fighting many battles in the Crusades, sat on this hill, put down his sword and shield and decided that he would fight no more. Looking at the extraordinary view from the summit he decided to become a hermit and grow grapes instead. A little chapel, dedicated to St Christopher the patron saint of travellers, has been built near the top of the hill on the spot where he laid down his sword. One of the finest French Syrahs is created from the vines close to this chapel, and the wine is called Hermitage La Chapelle. But especially fine Syrahs are cultivated in the local villages of Cornas and Saint-Joseph too.

It is also here in the northern Rhône that one of the world's greatest white wines is produced in tiny quantities. It is made from the Viognier grape variety and it is named after the village of Condrieu. Only about 30,000 cases of this nectar are produced each year, with low yields no higher than 41 hectolitres per hectare, ensuring high concentration and glycerol. This is one of my favourite white wines from France; it is completely different to the Viogniers in the Vins de Pays or elsewhere in the world, where the yields are higher and the flavour less intense. Condrieu has the most exotic fragrance and is a wonderfully opulent wine, brimming with seductive aromas of truffle, honeysuckle and hawthorn blossom, enhanced by mouth-watering flavours of apricot and peach that linger on an elegant finish. Barrel fermentation and around eight months on its lees gives the wine an extra layer of creamy and toasty complexity.

Moving down to the southern Rhône, the red wines are a blend of Syrah and Grenache grapes, along with small amounts of many others. The most famous wine is Châteauneuf-du-Pape, which under the Appellation rules is allowed to have thirteen different grape varieties in the blend, even a white grape. The best Châteauneufs are made from just the two main grapes, and the higher the proportion of Syrah the better.

These wines are big and powerful in good years, with huge amounts of character, tannin and flavour. What these wines lack in finesse and elegance is compensated for in immense structure and concentration. I prefer Gigondas, a hill village in the shadow of the Dentelles de Montmirail in Vaucluse, close to Mont Ventoux. This Jurassic limestone outcrop rises up like jagged horizontal teeth at the top of a hill. I tend to climb up to the summit of this hill and then rock-climb to the top of the Dentelles and look down at the amazing view of the surrounding vineyards. After which, in the summer, it is worth dining on the terrace of Les Florets restaurant, which is further down towards Gigondas, but still high enough to enjoy the spectacular view over a decent bottle of the local wine.

Cabernet Sauvignon is a grape which you can now find all over the world, but some of its greatest expressions are in Bordeaux in south-west France on the Gironde estuary, close to the Atlantic Ocean. Here it is warm in the summer, but sea breezes cool the grapes during the hottest days, so that the late-ripening Cabernet is fully ripened to perfection in the best years. Bordeaux has always been close to the

English heart since Eleanor of Aquitaine married Henry II in 1152, and we owned it, on and off, for the next 200 years!

The other important grape for red Bordeaux wines is Merlot. Cabernet Sauvignon is a small, thick-skinned grape which provides the wines with structure, tannins, blackcurrant fruit character and ageing ability. It prefers a well-drained, gravelly soil to create the finest, most distinguished wine, and this is found in the Médoc. The Merlot contributes the ballast, the mid-palate fleshy silkiness and smoothness, the soft, plump, ripe-fruit flavours together with good levels of alcohol and acidity. The blend of these two grape varieties complementing each other should provide the ingredients for a harmonious, complex and above all complete taste.

Broadly, the wines from the left bank are dominated by Cabernet, whilst the wines from the right bank are more focused on Merlot and Cabernet Franc, a cousin of the Cabernet Sauvignon grape. The great wines from the 1855 classification of Bordeaux on the left bank are found in the four communes stretching north in the Médoc from Margaux, just north of Bordeaux, through Saint-Julien, Pauillac and Saint-Estèphe. The wines tend to become more powerful as you travel north, more gentle wines in Margaux, more tannic wines in Saint-Julien, with many of the greatest wines in Pauillac and the most muscular powerful wines in Saint-Estèphe such as Château Montrose and Château Haut-Marbuzet. There are, of course, exceptions. Further north you find the Haut-Médoc and less fine wine, but lots of character and power, in wines such as the Cru Bourgeois Château Cissac.

In addition to the Cabernet and Merlot, smaller quantities of Cabernet Franc, Malbec and Petit Verdot have contributed to some very fine red wines which are exported all over the world.

Would I return to France for the finest Cabernets? Probably, is the answer, although this is a more difficult question, as the wines emanating from the Napa Valley in California made predominantly from the Cabernet Sauvignon grape are top-notch too, as the competitive tasting organised by Steven Spurrier showed in the "Judgement of Paris". Watch the film *Bottle Shock* if you are interested in this notorious blind wine-tasting competition. I have tasted some very fine first growths from Bordeaux together with the equivalent from Napa such as Stag's Leap, and I can only say that you'd have to be a purist to discount the American wines. It is not just in Napa, though, where Cabernets have been winning gold medals; I think the Cabernets from Napier in New Zealand, Barossa, McLaren Vale, Margaret River in Australia and Stellenbosch in South Africa are all different to Bordeaux, but at a normal, sensible price compete with reasonably priced claret.

It is the top wines from Bordeaux which have an authority and reputation, irrespective of their taste, with which the rest of the world cannot compete. The top first-growth brands of Château Margaux (Margaux), Château Latour, Château Lafite, Château Mouton-Rothschild (Pauillac) and Château Haut-Brion (Pessac-Léognan) all make exceptional wines each year, and with prices to match.

Bordeaux itself is a wonderful place to visit. There are a couple of restaurants which I would recommend. As usual, it is value that I am after, and the Mably restaurant is off the beaten track down a little side-street called Rue Mably. It is a little family-run affair; the food is delicious and very reasonably priced. La Cheminée Royale in Rue Saint-Rémi, where there are loads of restaurants lining the street, is superb, and also not expensive, and their steaks are cooked on an open fire in the restaurant *au feu de bois*. A decent glass of chilled lager cleanses the palate and refreshes the taste buds after a day of tasting and is a fine way to end a day's explorations in the vineyards.

There was one occasion when I was on a buying visit to Bordeaux, and I dined at Château Cissac in the Haut-Médoc. After a particularly good dinner with the owner and his daughter, the export director offered to show me the quickest way back into Bordeaux and told me to follow his car. It was pitch black and foggy outside in the early hours of the morning, so I accepted his offer of help with as much enthusiasm as I could manage at that stage in the evening.

I duly followed the car as it took me off into the forest along a little narrow lane. After about ten minutes I noticed that the car was speeding up ahead of me, so I put my foot down to keep up driving rather faster than I thought sensible but determined not to lose my shepherd. Soon I was travelling around bends at breakneck speed, and after a few more minutes of this white-knuckle ride the car ahead drove into a private drive, a figure rushed out of the car and ran towards the house and scuttled inside without a glance back at me. It was half-past one in the morning and I had no idea where I was, so I turned the car round and started back the way I had driven already. Eventually I found my way back into Bordeaux and fell into my hotel bed in the small hours.

The following morning at Château Cissac, a very traumatised and disgruntled cook arrived slightly late for work, explaining that she had been chased in her car by a mad Englishman the previous night, whom she had tried to shake off unsuccessfully. She had been terrified that I would attack her as she burst from her car and scuttled as fast as she could into her house.

I had followed the wrong car!

Soon after I joined the trade, I was in a Bordeaux restaurant with one of the owners of Château Palmer, Charlie Sichel, who has a very well-developed sense of humour. We ordered our main courses and I selected *steak frites* to go with the red wine we had smuggled into the restaurant. Having ordered, I expressed my concern that it was quite possible in France to be served horse meat as a steak instead of beef. I really didn't want to eat horse. Charlie said he thought it was unlikely. After our main courses arrived, I cut a slice of my steak, put it on my fork, adding a couple of chips for good measure, and was just about to put it into my mouth when across the table came the sound of "hee haw, hee haw, hee haw" and much laughter from Charlie.

There can be a huge amount of pretentiousness and snobbery in the wine world, which should be stopped at every opportunity. I heard a good story last time I was in Bordeaux about Anthony Barton, an Irishman who is known good-humouredly as "the bog frog", and who owns Château Léoville Barton. One day he was listening, as so often, to a visitor to the château who told him that he had so many great bottles in his cellar. The man had been going on and on about these great wines when finally Anthony apparently replied, *"What about buying a corkscrew?"* It is so often the image and the brand rather than the taste of the wine itself that engrosses people. I was told this story after telling the owner of Château Kirwan that I found it difficult to ever open a bottle of first growth if I was paying!

A short while ago I was invited to present a tutored wine tasting in Versailles at the Trianon Palace Hotel. The tasting took place in a private room, which was in fact used to rehearse the signing of the Treaty of Versailles after the war, before the actual signing in the palace next door. I gave the talk in English about French wine to a number of different nationalities including Germans, Danes and French people! I think it was at the end of this speech that I thought I had finally made it in the world of wine once and for all.

Soon after I joined the trade, my father couldn't make it to present an evening of French wines to an audience of accountants and lawyers in London. He asked me to present these wines in his absence and gave me a crib for each wine. It all went very well until, near the end, I was asked by one of the lawyers after we had tasted a Châteauneuf-du-Pape whether there was such a thing as a white Châteauneuf-du-Pape? I had a split second to decide my answer and, not knowing the actual answer, plumped for *"No there isn't such a thing!"*

"Hmm, that's strange," said the lawyer, *"I tasted a bottle of white Châteauneuf last week!"* At that moment I wanted the ground to swallow me up, but it taught me a lesson, which is that if you are not sure of the answer, it is better to be honest and admit it! It would be twenty years before I finally reached that audience in Versailles and answered all their questions confidently!

It was the esteemed Michael Broadbent, MW, author, auctioneer and wine critic, who wrote, *"A sight of the label is worth fifty years' experience."*

Whenever a particular wine colleague comes to supper, I tend to give him a "blind tasting". Curiously, when he arrives he normally darts straight for the kitchen and when I come in it is only to discover his nose deep inside my bin with his legs waggling in the air, upside down. On enquiring exactly what he is doing, I normally get a sheepish grin, and "I think I dropped my glasses" is the response. I've now taken to leaving the wrong bottle in the bin and enjoy listening to an authoritative explanation of how a Chardonnay from Chile is in fact a white Rioja from Spain. Very occasionally he gets his own back! Wine labels can often be quite confusing, but not in Alsace, where the grape variety *is* the name of the wine. Alsace is sometimes unfortunately overlooked as a serious quality wine-producing area. Many people associate its wines with Germany and may consequently believe them all to be light, fruity and sweet. The truth is they are not. Situated in the north-east of France, Alsace has a war-stricken history, belonging to Germany for many years. Alsace's present status as French dates from the treaty of Versailles after the 1914–18 war.

Alsace also has a unique climate caused by the protection of the Vosges mountains to the west of the vineyards. These mountains shelter the vines from the prevailing winds. Rainfall is incredibly low, since moist air forms into clouds as they cross the low flat lands of France from west to east and then deposit the rain on the Vosges, missing the vineyard region to the west of the Vosges. Rainfall is consequently incredibly low there. The average rainfall recorded in Colmar is 500 mm per year, the same as Jerez in southern Spain! You cannot argue with statistics, but the last time I visited Colmar it was absolutely pouring with rain!

All Alsace wines must be bottled where produced (a unique requirement for a still wine from France), and therefore authenticity is guaranteed. Alsatian wines combine the fruitiness of German wines with the dryness of French wines. Alsace guarantees a certain quality and style more surely than any other wine region. Rigorous identification of sites results in vines being planted on the land most suited to the vine. This is the secret behind the excellent quality of Alsatian wines. I think the thing I like most about them is their focus and concentration, probably the result of the low rainfall. This is coupled with the most incredibly intense aromatics and crisp acidity, which give these delicious wines a distinct and unique identity. My favourite Alsatian wine is Riesling, followed closely by dry Gewürztraminer and Pinot Gris. These wines finish with a tremendous length on the palate. Although most Alsace Rieslings are dry, they do make superb sweet late-harvest (*vendange tardive*) wines, due to the Rieslings being the last variety to ripen. The Muscat grape is a further delight if you enjoy a phenomenally perfumed bouquet. These Alsatian white wines certainly offer a delightful alternative to the ubiquitous Chardonnay and Sauvignon Blanc grape varieties.

After the samples are collected in my office in the UK, the wines are tasted on the tasting bench and compete in a form of musical chairs to see which one represents the best quality and value available from that region or grape variety. The trudging around and the tasting of so many wines whilst avoiding dangerous wildlife is well worth it when one finally comes across the jewel in the cellar.

I have been lucky enough to enjoy a number of memorable days with friends at Lord's, watching cricket and drinking some of the fruits of my labours, and I can only say that these occasions count as some of the happier moments of my life so far. Tasting a special tincture, remembering the vineyard and the story of the wine while watching cricket and chatting in the sunshine is sheer perfection. It probably wouldn't be a red wine from France, though, even with rare roast beef and horseradish sandwiches!

France still retains a very special place in the hearts of all wine lovers. Increasing competition from New World wine producers has ensured that French wines have improved in both quality and drinkability over the past decade. Even the French themselves recognise the attractive wine tastes emanating from emerging regions around the world. Tempus Alba wines from Argentina are now being imported by the French. On many French restaurant wine lists there is a section for *étrangers* wines. The quality of wine from Argentina, New Zealand, South Africa and Australia will only improve as the vines age. The only danger is that the climate in the warmer parts of the wine world will drive alcohol levels too high, but this will affect the warmer climes of France as well. The answer to the question of where most of the finest and most expensive wines are coming from today is still, ultimately, France, and I haven't seen Frog's Leap on a menu there yet.

The Marriage of Food and Wine

"A woman was sipping a glass of wine sitting on a terrace with her husband and she says, 'I love you so much, I don't know how I could live without you.' Her husband asks, 'Is that you or the wine talking?' She replies, 'It's me talking to the wine!'"

I love cooking with wine; sometimes I even add food!

It was Cicero who declared, *"The most fruitful of all the arts is the art of living well,"* and a major constituent of this is the art of eating and drinking well. Food and wine, like life itself, is a balancing act. Balance can be achieved, rather like a marriage, by pairing similar or contrasting flavours. Try a lightly sweet white wine with very spicy food or pair a high-acid wine with a high-acid dish.

A very nervous young man the night before his wedding asked his father what was the secret of a successful marriage. His father looked misty-eyed into the middle distance and mumbled that it was important to retain a little romance and excitement in the relationship. He suggested going out and watching a romantic film, sharing a candlelit dinner or enjoying some smoochy dancing. The father finished by saying, *"Your mother and I go out twice a week – she goes on a Tuesday and I go out on a Friday."*

Some wines just don't go with certain foods and the result can leave an unpleasant bitter and metallic taste in the mouth. This was graphically illustrated to me when I once went to a lecture on matching food and wine. My fellow students and I were asked to take a piece of smoked salmon on a slice of brown bread and chew on it for about a minute, before slurping some Crozes-Hermitage from the famous house of Jaboulet – a fine red Rhône wine. To my surprise, the wine tasted foul! It was lean, mean, horribly bitter and acidic. We were then all asked to chew on a piece of salami on bread for a minute and taste the *same* wine again. This time it tasted delicious. Red wine just does not go with raw fish, so sushi lovers beware! Smoked salmon, although an oily fish, is high in acids and salt. The tannin in red wine just does not mix, and the two flavours fight in the mouth. In fact, what actually happens is the tannin and acidity amplify each other.

Acidity will also neutralise acidity. I would advise pairing wines with high acidity with foods with high acidity. An example would be to drink Chablis, a Sauvignon Blanc or a dry Riesling, preferably from Germany – all wines with high and crisp acidity – with smoked salmon, which is also high in acidity. The wine should be chilled for half an hour in the fridge before opening, but the acids in the fish and wine will blend together in a sizzling piquancy which is a delight to the taste buds.

The matching of food and wine may be like a tempestuous marriage, perhaps hot and spicy but creating a fabulous blend. Spice and heat in food clashes with high alcohol. For the perfect blend for spicy dishes, look for wines with little or no oak and lower alcohol. A German Riesling springs to mind, a Sauvignon Blanc or, best of all, a Gewürztraminer, either sweet or dry but preferably from Alsace in France. The Gewürztraminer is spicy itself (*Gewürz* means spice in German) and goes beautifully with a spicy course.

One principle is to have simple food with fine wine. You don't want the ego of the chef to be fighting with the ego of the winemaker! For this reason, I always provide French bread, pâté, ham and cheese to accompany the wines on my wine courses.

There are three great lies in the world today: the first is "the cheque is in the post"; the second is "darling, I will still respect you in the morning"; and the third is "you cannot drink red wine with cooked fish!" The truth is lighter red wines with more marked acidity, such as Pinot Noir, do go very well with fish. A better rule would be: white with light and red with rich. Lighter meats such as chicken and pork will go well with heavier white wines such as Viognier and oaked Chardonnay. Preparation and sauce, though, are more important than what is being cooked; so if pork is put in a honey-and-mustard sauce the weight of the wine will need to be heavier and spicier to cope with the sauce.

Another principle of matching food and wine is to match the flavour of the wine with the flavour of the food. You may pair wine to food with specific flavour matches in a dish or perhaps think in terms of blocks of flavour. An example would be a mature New Zealand Sauvignon Blanc coupled with asparagus. As the Sauvignon Blanc grape ages, its flavour profile moves from intense gooseberry fruit and freshly cut grass character to literally tasting and smelling of asparagus. On the other hand, the grapefruit citrus flavours found in youthful old world Sauvignon Blanc go with fish for much the same reason that lemon is often served with fish. The flavours match each other perfectly. A sweet Gewürztraminer will pair perfectly with lychees, as the wine smells and tastes of the fruit.

A cool climate high-acid grape variety such as Sauvignon Blanc, Riesling or an unoaked, lean, crisp Chardonnay will each blend beautifully with fish in a rich creamy sauce. The principle is that the crisp acidity will cut through the oiliness of the fish but balance the texture of richness and fattiness in the sauce. The result is completely harmonious. Acid flavours like lemon or tomato need acidity in the wine.

Richness in a dish can also be matched with a rich wine. The wine should be full in flavour, so as not to taste lean in the mouth. A rich coq au vin would go beautifully with a rich, powerful Rhône blend, for example a Châteauneuf-du-Pape, Gigondas, Rhône Villlages or a Syrah/Shiraz from the New World.

Generally it's worth matching the intensity of flavour in the food to the weight or body of the wine. A heavy, alcoholic wine will not work with a delicate dish. If the food is delicate, choose a lighter or more elegant wine.

The tannins in red wines need to be handled carefully. Tannins make themselves known in the mouth by the roughness on the back of your teeth or a puckering sensation on the inside of your cheeks. Younger wines made from Cabernet Sauvignon tend to demonstrate this clearly.

Tannic wines should not really be drunk on their own. The chewy texture of meat, however, complements the rough taste of tannins and the combination again is a delight. But tannins will fight with salty dishes and can taste bitter.

Sweetness should be considered carefully when pairing wines with food. Sweet foods make dry red or white wine taste unpleasantly lean and acidic. Always finish your dry wine from the main course before you start pudding (I'm not convinced about the latest modern idea of drinking Shiraz with chocolate; it doesn't work for me), which will also give you the chance to move on to a sweet wine to go with a sweet pudding itself, which for me always enhances and adds something special to the final course.

Food and wine styles in any given region have usually evolved to complement each other. The strong but subtle flavours of Italian food blend with Italian wine. Good French wines have a finesse that complements the elegance of French cuisine. Equally food culture in regions which are close to the sea tend, unsurprisingly, to focus more on fish, and the wines of the local area have evolved to match that style of food. Inland regions, where historically it was almost impossible to eat fresh fish because of a lack of speedy transport, have developed gastronomy that is more in tune with meat and red wines.

This is why it is always preferable to ask, when eating in a restaurant in a wine region, what is the local food speciality which is recommended, and what is the preferred local wine to go with it. I have been surprised on many occasions whilst exploring new wine regions that the mix of a local food and wine is a perfect match, but in combinations which I would probably not normally have considered.

Fundamentally, drink wine to enjoy its taste, the company and the moment. The perfect food and wine pairing is elusive and somewhat mythical. Drink wine you like with food you like, but never stop experimenting. The marriage of food and wine should be a permanent affair.

Here are a few classic food and wine marriages made in heaven:

Gewürztraminer and Asian Spicy Food

The spicy grape variety Gewürztraminer has demonstrative lychee fruit character; this should be matched with any spicy dish, particularly a Chinese or Indian meal. The spiciness of both the wine and the food will create a wonderful mix in the mouth. I prefer the dry version of Gewürztraminer for this match, but sweet will blend well too.

Champagne and Strawberries

The acidity in the champagne mixes well with the acidity and sugar in the strawberries. Oysters are also notoriously a fabulous mix with champagne.

Muscadet Sur Lie with Shellfish

Muscadet from the Loire Valley, close to where the river runs into the sea at Nantes, has a very high acidity and is made from the Melon de Bourgogne grape variety. It is very lean and crisp with a light body. The better Muscadets are kept on their lees (dead yeast cells) in the vat and stirred up periodically to give the final wine a bready, yeasty flavour to blanket the acidity. White shellfish flesh is actually very rich, particularly in crab and lobster, so the acidity cuts through this richness perfectly.

Sancerre and Goat's Cheese

This is a traditional and classic combination; the gooseberry fruit character and high acidity from the Sancerre mixes beautifully with the creamy texture of the cheese.

Sauvignon Blanc and Asparagus

I like asparagus with lots of butter and pepper, and when accompanied by a glass of Sauvignon Blanc, with two or three years' age to it, it's a heavenly match. As the Sauvignon ages, so it actually develops an asparagus flavour of its own. The crisp acidity in the wine cuts through the butter and blends with the subtle flavour of capsicum.

Sauternes and Foie Gras

A sweet white wine such as Sauternes, or a Muscat de Beaumes de Venise, Monbazillac, Barsac or Muscat from Victoria in Australia, goes well with pretty well any pudding, but for me the finest match of all for sweet white wine is foie gras or a smooth pâté on toast. Although sweet wine appears soft, the sweetness conceals a high acidity which complements and cuts through the richness of the pâté. These wines will also go fabulously with Roquefort blue cheese, the spiciness and saltiness of the cheese blending magnificently with the sweetness of the wine.

Oaked Chardonnay and Roast Chicken

Chicken is pretty versatile, a lighter red wine such as Pinot Noir from New Zealand or for me a rich oaked Chardonnay from France or Australia all combine well. The caramel butterscotch flavour of the Chardonnay enhances the simple roast chicken. If the chicken is made with a mushroom or creamy sauce, then a more acidic red wine, such as a Chianti from Tuscany or a Pinot Noir from Burgundy. It is the sauce rather that the meat which really determines the wine.

Cabernet Sauvignon and Roast Lamb

Lamb is quite a fatty meat, while "left bank" Cabernet-dominated claret from Bordeaux can be quite austere and tannic in its youth. The texture of the tannins will cut through the richness and succulence of the lamb. The blackcurrant fruit character of the Cabernet also enhances the flavour of the lamb. It is not by accident that one of the finest clarets is called Château Mouton Rothschild. Bordeaux used to have an enormous number of sheep in the region.

Syrah and Pheasant

Most gamey meats such as venison, pheasant, pigeon, partridge, goose, rabbit and duck go extremely well with a Syrah from the Rhône valley

– with a little age. French Syrah, once aged, has quite an exotic spicy and peppery flavour of its own. As the grape ages, so farmyard flavours emerge which go beautifully with game.

Zinfandel and Pepper Steak

Zinfandel has a robust spicy and mildly peppery flavour of its own which matches the spiciness of the steak. The tannins are strong and the texture of the steak blend well with the tannins.

Australian Shiraz and Barbecue Meat

Sausages, steak, lamb chops and chicken drumsticks sizzled over a barbecue go beautifully with barrel-matured Australian Shiraz. The Shiraz should preferably be from the cooler climates of the Yarra Valley or Mornington Peninsula, but Barossa Shiraz goes well too. The concentration of ripe raspberry fruit and the smokiness of the oak balance the barbecue-charred and roasted flavours.

Châteauneuf-du-Pape and Casserole

The main principle is rich robust wine with rich robust food – this is perfect for a cold day in winter when you have been outside in freezing temperatures.

Chablis and Fish Pie

The zingy acidity in the Chablis cuts through and blends beautifully with the richness of the creamy and cheesy sauce in which the fish is served.

Côtes du Rhône and Shepherd's Pie

The lamb in the shepherd's pie, with its fattiness and smooth, buttery mashed potato, goes well with the tannins and the acidity of the Rhône wine, which cut through the stodginess of this comfort food. The good thing about Côtes du Rhône is that it is inexpensive and good value.

Fleurie and Charcuterie

The fruitiness and lightness of the Gamay, preferably a Beaujolais, mix well with the cold dryness of the meat, a dish which is often served with a fruit conserve.

A Pink Meal

Open a bottle of "pink fizz" with a high proportion of the Pinot Noir grape in the blend. Start with smoked salmon, move on to lobster and finish with strawberries. Or you could try a Tavel Rosé or a Sancerre Rosé instead of the fizz.

Port and Stilton

This is another classic example of the salt-and-sweet marriage. The tannins in normal red wine will fight saltiness, so the sweetness and weight of the alcohol in port mix well with the salty cheese.

In Appendix (1) there is a fuller listing of starters and main courses coupled with recommended grape varieties to go with each dish.

Finally, what goes with parrot? I am reminded of the story of the man who inherited a parrot which hurled abuse at him from the moment he entered his house. Eventually the man became so angry that he dumped the parrot in the deep-freeze. Even more shrieking was followed by whines and finally silence. After about five minutes the man opened the deep freeze and the parrot very slowly and carefully stepped out and said, *"I am very very sorry, I won't be rude or abusive ever again, I promise. Please forgive me… and, er, may I ask you what exactly the chicken did?"*

"To pontificate, to let opinions rule your appreciation of wine and to be unable to feel, as the candles gutter and the moon rises on a warm summer night, that the wine on the table, however unsung and lacking in renown is, for that short moment, perfection itself, is to miss the whole heart of wine – and of life too."
Oz Clarke

An Englishman's home is his carafe! The horrific cost of wine in restaurants with the 300–400% mark-up on a bottle is increasingly encouraging wine lovers to stay at home and take up their corkscrew in protest.

I have discovered during these straitened times that clients are prepared to pay a little more for a decent bottle to enjoy at home, but still reckoning that it is a quarter of the price one would have had to pay for the same bottle in a restaurant. The saving on the wine alone probably pays for the food! These are wines to dine for!

One of the questions I am often asked on my wine courses is whether it is really necessary to decant wine.

The food needs preparation before the dinner party, and so too does the wine. Even top-quality white wines should be decanted. Most importantly, any red wine to go with your fish course or the main course should be decanted for about an hour unless it is a very old wine which is going to die in your glass after 15 minutes breathing oxygen.

Even champagne should be allowed a little breathing time before drinking. The original reason for decanting was to ensure that the sediment didn't get into your glass. In the old days before we had today's aggressive filtration methods, a wine would naturally throw a considerable sediment. Decanting was simply used to separate the clear wine from the sediment dregs. Nowadays there is less sediment in bottles, so the need is reduced.

Have you ever noticed how, if by some accident you don't manage to finish a bottle of red during the evening, the following day, when you try the second half of the bottle, it tastes much better than the night before? The reason is the wine has breathed for twenty-four hours, broadened out and is finally showing its best side. In my view it is essential to decant all red wine, since they need to breathe, and pouring the wine into a jug will help it oxidise and breathe after months or years cooped up in a bottle. The act of decanting just gives the wine more aeration and helps the wine to show off its bouquet and character better. The oxygen opens up the wine, helping it to age in the glass or decanter and soften the hard tannic edges and break down lean mean acidity.

You don't need some smart decanter to carry this out – any water jug will do. Splashing the wine into the jug will help aerate the wine further. There was one occasion when a friend invited me to enjoy a delicious bottle of 1986 Château Ducru Beaucaillou and we did not have a jug or a decanter to use. In the end I resorted to using a cafetière, but without the plunger!

Even white wine should be decanted occasionally. However, the only wines this really applies to are the great white Burgundies that are opened whilst young. The aeration and oxygenation helps the flavours to emerge more quickly, so the true complexity of the wine can be enjoyed. The lean sharp acidity in a great young white wine can sometimes conceal the fruit and character behind. A little time in the decanter will soften this and help the more subtle flavours emerge. I opened a fine Puligny-Montrachet recently which was only three years old and tasted it immediately after opening to find that its harsh acidity concealed the green flavours of youth. I decanted the wine, and after an hour in the jug it had softened and some of the wine's complexity began to come through, with flavours of honey, vanilla cream and nuts and the sumptuous, heady aroma which is unique to Puligny.

My rule of thumb is that an hour in the decanter equates to about a year of maturing in bottle.

A few years ago in Napa, I came across a new contraption called a Vinturi Wine Aerator, which immediately aerates wine as though it had been in a decanter for an hour. This is a device shaped like a funnel with small holes in the side so that as the wine falls through the funnel air is sucked into the wine. In my experience it does soften the tannins of firm structured reds, but I would only use it in an emergency. It is still preferable to use a jug for an hour if there is time.

If you take the cork out of the bottle and leave it to stand there will be very little effect on the wine at all, since only a tiny amount of oxygen is getting into the wine through the neck of the bottle. You could leave the bottle out for hours and the effect on the wine would be negligible.

What about glasses? Should you have special glasses for champagne, white and red wines? The most important consideration when choosing glasses for serving any type of wine is to make sure that the bowl of the glass is wider than the entrance to the glass. This is so the aromatics of the wine can be concentrated at the rim of the glass and one can detect more intensity from the "nose" of the bouquet. The perfect-shaped glass is actually a brandy balloon with its very narrow entrance and broad bowl at the bottom. I have sometimes used brandy balloons for serving wine. I have happy memories of drinking red wine from such a glass in front of a blazing log fire at home with my parents.

This principle of a narrow entrance and a wider bowl to the glass should apply to all wines, including champagne. I do sometimes show off with my favourite champagne glasses, which have hollow stems but open outwards rather than trapping the aromas in the lip of the glass. The reason is purely to delight my eyes, as the bubbles rise up through the stem. I love my Edwardian champagne glasses, which were allegedly originally moulded to the shape of the breasts of Marie Antoinette. This was the traditional way of serving champagne before a method was devised to clear the liquid of all the gunk generated by the secondary fermentation in the bottle. The old dead yeast cells would drop down to the bottom of the hollow stem, so that the rest of the liquid would remain pristine.

153

I am prepared to eschew some of the nose of the champagne because the look of the glass appeals to me. However, on one occasion, while I was a guest of Roederer in Rheims, I was told in no uncertain terms that a normal wine glass with a wide bowl and a narrower entrance should really be used, so as to collect and amplify all the scents from the liquid. It certainly made the vintage Cristal taste even better, with its fresh crisp purity and opulent nuances of brioche and cream dancing on the tongue.

I also like my red-wine glasses to be fairly big, since the liquid will breathe more easily in a larger bowl, revealing more of the wine's character. It also enables me to tell my doctor that I only have a glass or two each day. He doesn't need to know that each glass holds about a bottle...

White wines are generally served in glasses with stems, so that while you are holding the stem you are not warming the glass with your hand. There is nothing worse than a lukewarm glass of champagne or white wine. Equally for red wine, if served too cold, it is possible to sit the bowl of the glass on top of one's hand, with the stem in between one's fingers, so that the palm of your hand warms the liquid.

Serving wine at the correct temperature at a dinner party is also important. There is nothing worse than serving a fine white wine so cold that it is like an iced lolly and impossible to taste. Unless of course it happens to be a dull, cheap concoction from the supermarket, in which case the colder the better! Just cool is fine for a decent white wine, so that it is possible to taste all the flavours. The overriding objective should be to maintain this temperature as the wine warms or cools in your glass, dependent on the time of year.

In the same way that there are some people who believe red wine should never be served with fish, there are some who believe that red wine should never be served cool. This depends entirely on the weather and the type of red in my view. If it is lunchtime on a hot summer's day, a chilled youthful bottle of red wine made from the Gamay grape is a delight. Gamay produces wines with intense, concentrated red cherry fruits and reacts well to being chilled. Some argue that a Pinot Noir is also worth chilling in similar circumstances. I think that I would only chill these wines if they are very young and not expensive. If a wine is just displaying simple primary fruit in its youth, chilling it is fine; the acidity feels refreshing. However, once a red wine starts to develop secondary characters such as tobacco and farmyard flavours, I think chilling is not such a good idea.

Red wines with firm tannins made, for example, from the Syrah, Cabernet Sauvignon or Malbec grape, should not be chilled, as the tannins will taste more pronounced and bitter when cooled.

Entertaining at home for dinner can sometimes present problems with regard to which wines should be chosen to go with which course. If your budget allows I would still recommend always starting with fizz.

Little-known but extremely tasty non-vintage champagnes shouldn't cost the earth. A good-value alternative to champagne is crémant from France, which is made in the same way as champagne but at about half the price. Crémant de Bourgogne is a style which is attractive and economical and, it is claimed, was made before champagne existed. Prosecco is an even cheaper option, but not made in the same expensive way as champagne. If you want to show off, Pol Roger, Bollinger or

Krug non-vintage champagnes are all exceedingly good. As for the best, then in my opinion you have to select vintage Krug.

Increasingly, I find white wine or rosé is served as an aperitif. For white wines and indeed reds to drink on their own, or with nibbles as an aperitif, I would recommend New World wines rather than Old. This is generally because the tannin and acidity in these wines tends to be less austere. Old World wines were made to drink with food, so that the acidity or tannin cuts through and blends with the richness of the food. I like to drink softer New World Sauvignon Blanc as an aperitif. Sometimes a young Sauvignon Blanc on its own can be very acidic, so I like the Edwards Vineyard Sémillon Sauvignon from Margaret River, since the Sémillon grape softens and adds interest to the blend, giving it mid-palate ballast. It is delicious on its own or with crisps. If you're eating nuts, cashews in particular, I prefer a New World lightly oaked Chardonnay, which often displays a subtle nuttiness itself. The Wedgetail Chardonnay from the Yarra Valley in Australia or Staete Landt Chardonnay from Marlborough in New Zealand are almost too good for this but drink well, again on their own, or with nuts. As a cost-effective and different alternative, I would recommend a chilled glass of Manzanilla or Fino Sherry, which, although out of fashion, are both incredibly delicious. With enormous flavour and bone-dry, this fortified wine gets those juices running and makes you feel hungry.

For a starter, I would suggest a dry white Burgundy as a fine, polished, classy accompaniment to anything which isn't too spicy. You could go for top-notch white Burgundy, or less well known but rather good is a Saint-Aubin. Even more cost-effective, from a few miles further south in the Côte Chalonnaise, are the villages of Montagny,

Rully, Mercurey and Givry, which all produce fine, lightly oaked wines which are similar to, but displaying slightly less depth than, the great expensive Côte de Beaune white wines. Again, if the budget is constrained, go for a simple Bourgogne Blanc. All these wines are made in Burgundy using the Chardonnay grape, and you'll notice a subtle hint of vanilla and caramel on the nose, which is created by ageing the wine in new oak barrels.

You could always go for purity as an aperitif, a Petit Chablis or a Chablis Premier Cru, both of which are made from the Chardonnay grape variety but are unoaked and deliciously dry and crisp. Perfect with a smoked salmon starter.

If the starter is spicy, I would recommend a Sauvignon Blanc. Top notch would be Sancerre. Mid-price would be a New Zealand Sauvignon such as Fiddler's Green in Waipara or the Edwards Vineyard Sauvignon from Margaret River in Australia. If you are on a tight budget I would advise a good-value oaked Sémillon Sauvignon and Muscadelle blend such as Cuvée Clémence from Bordeaux.

For the main course, if you are serving a light white meat such as chicken, turkey, duck, partridge, fish or pork, a lighter red wine made from the Pinot Noir grape is the best option. Expensive: go for a red Burgundy such as Chambolle-Musigny (more elegant with smoother tannins) or Gevrey-Chambertin (more gutsy, big and powerful). I would also encourage you to try one of the two best South African Pinots, which in my view are Bouchard Findlayson's Pinot Noir or Meerlust Pinot Noir. Mid-price I would recommend a Pinot from California – Cuvaison is a favourite – or Wedgetail Estate from the cool Yarra Valley region of Australia. For the less expensive try a Pinotage from South Africa – my favourite is the Mooiplaas Pinotage – or a Bourgogne Pinot Noir for an entry-level red Burgundy. Monthélie is another underrated, less expensive but high-quality earthy red Burgundy.

If the next course is with darker meats such as beef or lamb or a stew with a rich sauce of some kind, you are now into Cabernet, Malbec and Syrah/Shiraz territory.

Expensive: a top 10–20-year-old claret such as Château Palmer, a top Shiraz from Australia such as Grange or Brini Estate Sebastian Shiraz from McLaren Vale or a Hermitage from northern Rhône. Alternatively, I would advise a top reserve Malbec from Bodega Salentein, Tempus Alba or Enrique Foster.

Mid-range: Crozes-Hermitage, Château Angludet or Château Haut-Marbuzet, Margaret River Edwards Vineyard Cabernet or Hawkes Bay Cabernet from 5–10 years ago. A Malbec from Argentina – my favourite good-value one is from the Tempus Alba vineyard.

Inexpensive: any *petit château* from a great year in Bordeaux, particularly from Blaye or Bourg. My favourite good-value Merlot-dominated château from Blaye is Château Bellevue-Gazin, and the 2009 vintage is superb. A simple Côtes du Rhône is also terrific value, inexpensive and rarely disappoints.

With cheese: pretty well any red will go with cheese. I rather like having powerful Italian wines made either from the Sangiovese or Nebbiolo grape. These wines are notorious for having high levels of both acidity and tannin and will cut through the richness of the cheese. The important thing is not to have blue cheese with red wine, as the salt in the cheese can sometimes react against the tannins, leaving a bitter taste in the mouth. The other wine I love to put with cheese is a big, robust southern Rhône.

With pudding, obviously a sweet wine should be served, and the wine needs to be sweeter than the food, otherwise the wine will taste slightly sour and mean. Sauternes is the top style; if you want the best it would be the famous Château d'Yquem. Here the grapes are picked by hand – not by the bunch, only by the individual grape, once the noble rot has set in the autumn. My favourite better-value Sauternes is Château Climens, which on my last tasting of about 100 Sauternes came out as close in quality to Yquem, and is made in the same way as Yquem, but at less than half the price. Something even better value is the second wine of Climens called Cyprès de Climens.

A mid-price option for me would be a Muscat Beaumes de Venise or a Hungarian Tokay with as many puttonyos as you can afford. Less expensive sweet alternatives would be Muscats from Australia, or try a Monbazillac from France.

With coffee, of course, the perfect accompaniment is just decent conversation, and I often find that at this stage in proceedings I have become incredibly knowledgeable on virtually any subject you care to mention!

How much wine should you serve per head? This partly depends on how many are driving and whether it is mid-week or not. As a rule of thumb I work on the basis of a bottle a head, with a spare in case of need. The most important thing is to ensure that none of the glasses of your guests who are not driving fall to low tide. I am always happy to drive home after a dinner party on the proviso that my wife isn't going to be able to drive at the end of the evening. There is nothing worse than depriving oneself of delicious claret through a dinner in order to drive soberly, only to find that my wife is also totally sober. What a waste. It reminds me of the story of a police patrol who were keeping watch for drink-drivers one night at a renowned local pub. Late in the evening, the officer noticed a man leaving the bar so intoxicated that he could barely walk. The man stumbled around the car park for a few minutes with the officer quietly watching…

After what seemed an eternity and trying his keys in five different vehicles, the man managed to find his own car, into which he fell. He was there for a few minutes as a number of other patrons left the bar and drove off. Finally he started his car, switched the wipers on and off (it was a dry night), flicked the hazard flasher on and off, tooted the horn and then switched on the lights. He moved the vehicle forward a few inches, reversed a little and then remained stationary for a few more minutes as more patrons left in their vehicles…

At last he pulled out of the car park and started to drive slowly down the street. The police officer, having patiently waited all this time, now started up his patrol car, put on the flashing lights, promptly pulled the man over and carried out a breathalyser test. To his amazement, the breathalyser indicated no evidence that the man consumed alcohol at all. Dumbfounded, the officer said, *"I'll have to ask you to accompany me to the police station. This breathalyser equipment must be broken."*

"I doubt it," said the man. *"Tonight I'm the designated decoy."*

As an after-dinner speaker I now find myself totally sober at the coffee stage with full glasses of the wines in front of me that everyone else has been enjoying during the meal with each course. It is at this moment in the evening when I am beginning to feel a little nervous in preparation for standing on my feet to speak for half an hour.

I remember one occasion when I went over to Guernsey to speak in St Peter Port. The organisers told me that I would be speaking after the president of the association had said a few words before me. At 10.30 p.m. the President stood up and gave a twenty-minute speech on the state of the association, followed by a twenty-minute speech from the Prime Minister of Guernsey on the state of the nation, followed by a twenty minute speech from the Chancellor of Guernsey on the state of the finances of Guernsey. At 11.30 p.m., having listened to an hour of speeches, the state of the audience was totally comatose, and it was then I was called upon to speak. Everyone seemed to be snoring and/or keeling over; a few had actually gone to sleep. I'd been drinking a lot of coffee over the past hour to keep myself awake. I spoke from somewhere near the ceiling, full of caffeine, and gave it all I had until midnight. This is clearly a job for insomniacs.

I remember the very first after-dinner speech I gave was in London, curiously in the cellars at Berry Bros. & Rudd in St James's. I sat next to the host and senior partner of a city law firm, who, just before he stood up to introduce me, leaned over towards me and asked if I was ready to speak. He told me that at the annual dinner the year before he had invited Geoff Miller, the celebrated England cricketer, Chairman of the England Cricket Selectors and well-known after-dinner speaker to address their annual dinner. *'He was the best speaker we've ever had... so witty and amusing – I mean really, very funny indeed. Now, are you ready, Graham?'* I suddenly felt very unready indeed!

Whether you are going out to dinner or you are hosting a dinner at home, the point is to enjoy the moment with good food, fine wine and excellent company, all of which will put life's troubles firmly into perspective.

"Each year the roots dig deeper to produce wines of increasing complexity, which in bottle will mature for another generation, immune to all the madness which man seems condemned to create for himself."
Peter Sichel

The highest price ever paid for a bottle of wine to date is £191,000, for a six-litre bottle, called a methuselah (named after a biblical patriarch who lived to the age of 969), of Château Cheval Blanc 1947.

The highest price paid for a standard 75-centilitre single bottle was an 1869 Château Lafite, which was auctioned in Hong Kong for £146,000. That equates to £18,250 per glass and £1,260 per sip. The most expensive white wine ever sold was a 200-year-old bottle of Château d'Yquem 1811 for £75,000.

The most interesting bottle ever sold was a Château Lafite 1887, which was auctioned for around £100,000, on the basis that it was reputed to have been owned by Thomas Jefferson, America's third

President (who signed the Declaration of Independence). Benjamin Wallace wrote a book called *Billionaire's Vinegar*, which sheds further light on the story and questions whether the bottle really was the property of Thomas Jefferson. It would certainly be vinegar if it was opened now, but its value lies not in the taste but in its collectability.

One of the questions I often encounter is, *"What is your favourite wine?"*

This is a very difficult question to answer, since it rather depends on the circumstances. A wine which I would enjoy on a cold winter's night in front of a crackling log fire will be different to the favourite wine I would choose for a picnic lunch on a warm summer's day. It also depends what I am going to be eating with it, as there are many wines I would not drink on their own. Often, I particularly appreciate wines which remind me of happy moments in my life.

As discussed before, sometimes wine can take us back, enable us to remember and relive that experience and dream that dream again.

I am often contacted by clients who have visited one of the little vineyards scattered across the globe which I represent in the UK. The Tempus Alba vineyard in Mendoza is a good example, as it is easy to visit, being one of the closest vineyards to the centre of Mendoza. It is a beautiful estate, a charming vineyard to visit on your holidays in Argentina. The view from the roof terrace over the vineyards towards the majestic snow-capped Andes mountains in the distance is truly magnificent. Once you have tasted a glass of Malbec in the sunshine looking at this spectacle it is never forgotten. When you arrive home you want to relive the dream again, and drinking that Malbec gives even more fulfilment and satisfaction in knowing the vineyard and recognising the memory.

Château Angludet in Margaux in Bordeaux will always be close to my heart, because of the happy times and warm friendships forged in the hard-labour camp that was the picking of the vintage. It is also a wonderful wine with amazing balance, concentration and intensity. Add the memories of the 1983 harvest and the wine becomes unique and very special to me.

One of my favourite white wines is Gewürztraminer from Germany or Alsace, and indeed there are some serious examples coming out of New Zealand and Australia. The wine is intensely aromatic; it smells of lychees and roses and is one of the easiest wines to pick out in a blind tasting just on the nose. Often sweet, I prefer a dry style of "Gewürz" – which is the perfect accompaniment to a hot curry. It was my wife's favourite white wine when I first met her, and I can remember ordering a bottle in a restaurant on the Île Saint-Louis in Paris soon after we were married. Unusually, we decided to order a second bottle to fortify us for the walk back to our hotel. When we arrived at the hotel, we decided rather foolishly to finish the evening with a nightcap. So I ordered a couple of brandies at the bar and then we decided it was time to go dancing. I discovered what I deduced was a ballroom in the hotel with what appeared to be a dance floor at one end and lots of people milling around enjoying themselves. So I took Nicola in my arms and we danced... Oh how we danced; all inhibitions gone, we really let ourselves go. I've never strutted my stuff in quite such an enthusiastic way on a dance floor since, well, almost never. It was while we were dancing that I started to realise that there weren't many other people on the dance floor with us. This was followed by the gradual realisation that there was actually nobody dancing except us and some bloke on his own at one side of the dance floor. It then finally dawned on me that there were a lot of people all staring at us from the other side of the room. When I spotted the lectern and the surprised and amused look on the face of the man staring intently at us, it finally dawned on me that this wasn't a dance floor at all. It was in fact a room which had been hired for a business lecture and the lecturer had just stopped giving his talk from behind a lectern to an audience of a few hundred people. We had mistakenly barged in on a seminar, and as we hastily ran off the raised stage from which the lecture was being presented, I can still remember the professor saying to us as we passed him heading for the door, *"Young love…. so cute!"* to a certain amount of mirth and laughter from the audience. Whenever I drink Gewürztraminer now I am reminded of that special memorable evening in Paris, and despite such embarrassment, this wine is still one of my favourite whites. It is the memories that so often contrive to evoke pleasure from a particular wine.

The Syrah grape variety is a favourite of mine. It produces its finest wines in the northern Rhône, around the granite hill of Hermitage on the east bank of this great river. It is thought that the Syrah was first planted in the Rhône over two thousand years ago by the Persians travelling from Shiraz. It is mentioned in the writings of Pliny. In my view, the greatest Syrah vines are grown on this hill. As discussed earlier, there is a small chapel near the summit today which overlooks the Rhône valley dedicated to St Christopher – the patron saint of travellers. The most famous wine created from the vines around this chapel is known as Hermitage la Chapelle, and that is probably my favourite wine. During the 18th and 19th centuries the great wines of Bordeaux such as Château Lafite, Latour, Margaux and Haut-Brion were "doctored" with a little Hermitage to give them more colour, structure and oomph. On some labels the wine was even marketed as being *Hermitagé*. I remember after a long tasting one morning, soon after I had joined the wine trade, I climbed this hill with my father. We climbed up together discussing the wines we had tasted that morning and plans for the future. We arrived at the top and sat down with a simple baguette filled with cheese, ham and lettuce, and while we chewed and talked we enjoyed the wonderful view across the valley and the great river running in the distance along the valley floor.

In the winter, on a cold evening, Hermitage is perfect when drunk with some game, or perhaps a fillet of venison. As far as I am concerned, it probably is the best Syrah in the world (Grange from Australia will just have to forgive me), and whenever I am lucky enough to drink it, I remember the long walk up to the chapel and the wonderful view over the enchanting Rhône valley where I once sat and ate a simple cheese and ham baguette with my dad.

So to conclude, *carpe vinum*, as we like to say in the Dead Bottles Society, let the laughter and pleasure created by drinking a particular wine become the music of your soul.

***

You can watch *The Wine Explorer's Three Minute Wine Guide* on YouTube at: youtu.be/tAj-zqnndy8

All you need to know about wine in three minutes, or fewer than 500 words. As Henry VIII said to his wives, I won't keep you long.

Wine is like art and music. Its appreciation is hugely subjective and personal; it is all about individual preference. You might like Keane and Picasso, whereas I prefer Coldplay and Caravaggio. Wine is the same, it is just a matter of taste.

Do you like the flavour of gooseberries? Try Sauvignon Blanc. Do you prefer blackcurrants? Try Cabernet Sauvignon. Wine is simply fermented grape juice – in the Northern Hemisphere it is colder, and therefore grapes are not as ripe as those grown in the heat of the summers in the Southern Hemisphere, like Australia and South Africa. More of the acidity in grapes grown in the heat of the Southern Hemisphere sunshine is converted into sugar, so that during fermentation, when the yeasts gobble up that sugar it is converted into higher levels of alcohol. The wines produced from these warmer climates are therefore bigger, richer wines with higher alcohol and lower natural acidity. The wines from Germany or England in the generally cooler northern climate are conversely lighter, crisper, more acidic lower-alcohol wines, sometimes as low as 8%, whereas in South Africa the natural alcohol level can rise to higher than 15%.

How can you tell quality in a wine faced with just a glass? Michael Broadbent said that a glance at the label is worth fifty years' experience – so without that benefit, what determines quality? The answer is balance, harmony and intensity of flavour. Wine is made up of fruit, acid, tannin and alcohol – if one of these is out of kilter with the others

— too much tannin, a roughness on the inside of the cheeks, or too much alcohol and dumpiness on the finish, then the wine is not such good quality, as it is not in balance.

But if the fruit is intense and concentrated with tannins, acidity and alcohol all harmoniously knitted together, then you have a wine that sings to you with real quality.

What do you search for in a vineyard if you're looking for a seriously good wine? As Jeremy Clarkson might say, we're looking for a Ferrari in a bottle for the price of a Škoda. The key factor is the age of the vine — the older the better. The older the vine the fewer grapes are produced, but the finer the quality. Older vines of thirty years or more produce the finest, most characterful, concentrated and intense flavours. Wine improves with age; I like it more the older I get. As Hugh Johnson said, the point of drinking wine is to drink what thrills you. This is true: it's all about your personal taste.

Happiness is a bottle uncorked… You can watch this and many other videos on the Wine Explorer's YouTube channel: youtu.be/b5HGI3JUiaw.

So what is the secret of a long, happy life?

A woman walked up to a little old man rocking in a chair on his porch. *"I couldn't help noticing how happy you look,"* she said. *"What's your secret for a long happy life?"*

"I smoke three packets of cigarettes a day," he said. *"I also drink a case of port and a case of claret a week, eat fatty foods and never exercise."*

"That's amazing," the woman replied. *"How old are you?"*

"Twenty-six," he said.

I'll be happy when... when will we be happy?

We convince ourselves that life will be better after we get married, have a baby, drink a bottle and then another. Then we are frustrated that the kids aren't old enough and we'll be more content when they are.

After that, we're frustrated that we have teenagers to deal with, which drives us to the bottle.

We will certainly be happy when they are out of *that* stage.

We tell ourselves that our life will be complete when our spouse gets his or her act together, when we get a smarter car, when we are able to go on a nice holiday or when we retire.

The truth is there's no better time to be happy than right now.

If not now, when?

Your life will always be filled with challenges.

It's best to admit this to yourself and decide to be happy anyway.

Happiness is the way.

So, treasure every moment and every bottle that you have, and treasure it more because you shared the wine with someone special, special enough to spend your time with... and remember that time waits for no one.

So, stop waiting...

Until your car or mortgage is paid off.

Until you get a new car or home.

Until your kids leave the house.

Until you go back to school.

Until you finish school.

Until you lose 10lbs.

Until you gain 10lbs.

Until you get married.

Until you get a divorce.

Until you have kids.

Until you retire.

Until summer.

Until spring.

Until winter.

Until autumn.

Until you die.

There is no better time than right now to be happy.

Happiness is a journey, not a destination.

So work like you don't need money, love like you've never been hurt and dance like no one's watching.

Happy days.

Appendix 1: Food and Wine: Starters

Starter	Recommendation	Second Recommendation
Antipasti	Marsala	Sémillon
Avocado with Crab	Riesling	Chenin Blanc
Avocado with Prawns	Riesling	Chenin Blanc
Bacon, Avocado & Chicken Salad	Oaked Chardonnay	Sauvignon Blanc
Baked Italian Sausage	Gamay	Barbera
BBQ Rack Ribs	Syrah	Shiraz
Beef Carpaccio	Gamay	Barbera
Beef Jerky	Shiraz	Syrah
Blinis	Sparkling Shiraz	Unoaked Chardonnay
Bouillabaisse	Pinot Noir	Rosé
Breaded Mushrooms	Oaked Chardonnay	Sangiovese
Bruschetta	Melon de Bourgogne	Chenin Blanc
Canapés	Unoaked Chardonnay	Riesling
Caesar Salad	Sauvignon Blanc	Oaked Chardonnay
Cajun Prawns	Gewürztraminer	Riesling
Calamari	Sauvignon Blanc	Chenin Blanc
Caramelised Onion Tart	Dry Riesling	Chardonnay
Carrot & Coriander Soup	Oaked Chardonnay	Riesling
Cheese & Spinach Tart	Unoaked Chardonnay	Pinot Grigio
Cheese Fondue	Dry Riesling	Sangiovese
Chicken Goujons	Oaked Chardonnay	Pinot Grigio
Chicken Liver & Pancetta Pâté	Sweet White	Sauvignon Blanc
Chicken Liver Parfait	Sweet White	Pinot Grigio
Chicken Liver Pâté	Sweet White	Pinot Noir
Chicken Soup	Sangiovese	Oaked Chardonnay
Chicken Tikka Skewers	Dry Riesling	Syrah
Chicken Wings	Pinot Noir	Barbera

Starter	Recommendation	Second Recommendation
Chinese Dumplings	Gewürztraminer	Riesling
Club Salad	Oaked Chardonnay	Pinot Grigio
Crab Claws	Chenin Blanc	Melon de Bourgogne
Crab Crostini	Sauvignon Blanc	Chenin Blanc
Crab Fishcakes	Melon de Bourgogne	Pinot Noir
Crayfish & Smoked Salmon Cocktail	Unoaked Chardonnay	Sauvignon Blanc
Deep-Fried Camembert	Pinot Noir	Merlot
Dim Sum	Gamay	Riesling
Dolmades	Gewürztraminer	Riesling
Dressed Crab	Melon de Bourgogne	Chenin Blanc
Duck & Orange Pâté	Sweet White	Pinot Noir
Duck & Port Pâté	Sweet White	Sangiovese
Duck Confit	Pinot Noir	Sangiovese
Egg Mayonnaise	Riesling	Unoaked Chardonnay
Fish Pâté	Sweet wine	Spanish Cava
Fish Soup	Pinot Noir	Merlot
Garlic & Cheese Dough Balls	Pinot Noir	Sangiovese
Garlic Bread	Pinot Noir	Barbera
Garlic Mushrooms	Grenache	Riesling
Goat's Cheese & Beetroot Fondue	Sauvignon Blanc	Pinot Grigio
Goat's Cheese & Red Onion Tart	Sauvignon Blanc	Pinot Grigio
Goat's Cheese Brûlée	Sauvignon Blanc	Pinot Grigio
Grapefruit Cocktail	Pinot Blanco	Sauvignon Blanc
Green Salad	Riesling	Pinot Blanc
Lamb Koftas	Cabernet Sauvignon	Syrah
Leek & Potato Soup	Syrah	Sangiovese
Melon	Unoaked Chardonnay	Chenin Blanc
Melon Balls with Smoked Ham	Riesling	Catawba
Meze	Viognier	Rosé
Minestrone Soup	Syrah	Merlot
Moules Marinière	Melon de Bourgogne	Sauvignon Blanc

Starter	Recommendation	Second Recommendation
Mushroom & Stilton Brioche	Sweet White	Merlot
Mushroom Soup	Pinot Noir	Barbera
Mushroom Tart	Grenache	Sangiovese
Mushrooms al Forno	Grenache	Sangiovese
Mushrooms in Roquefort Sauce	Gewürztraminer	Pinot Noir
Nachos	Riesling	Barbera
Nut Mix	Viognier	Oaked Chardonnay
Octopus Terrine	Unoaked Chardonnay	Chenin Blanc
Olives	Viognier	Pinot Blanc
Oriental Duck Spring Roll	Pinot Noir	Riesling
Oxtail Soup	Syrah	Malbec
Oysters	Melon de Bourgogne	Chenin Blanc
Pea & Ham Soup	Oaked Chardonnay	Viognier
Pear, Roquefort and Spinach Salad	Sauvignon Blanc	Gewürztraminer
Poached Salmon	Pinot Noir	Oaked Chardonnay
Pork & Apricot Terrine	Sweet White	Sangiovese
Potato Gnocchi	Riesling	Gewürztraminer
Potato Skins	Sauvignon Blanc	Merlot
Potato Wedges	Riesling	Gamay
Prawn Cocktail	Unoaked Chardonnay	Chenin Blanc
Radish Confit	Riesling	Sauvignon Blanc
Salmon Fishcake	Pinot Noir	Oaked Chardonnay
Sautéed Foie Gras	Riesling	Semillon
Savoury Biscuits	Syrah	Montilla
Scotch Broth	Syrah	Merlot
Seared King Scallops	Sauvignon Blanc	Chenin Blanc
Smoked Chicken Salad	Oaked Chardonnay	Pinot Noir
Smoked Mackerel Pâté	Sauvignon Blanc	Riesling
Smoked Salmon	Unoaked Chardonnay	Sauvignon Blanc
Spanish Tapas	Cava	Torrontés
Spicy Aromatic Chicken	Riesling	Gewürztraminer
Spinach & Cheese Dip	Pinot Noir	Rosé

Starter	Recommendation	Second Recommendation
Steamed Clams	Melon de Bourgogne	Chenin Blanc
Stuffed Mushrooms	Merlot	Viognier
Stuffed Pepper	Viognier	Riesling
Sushi	Chenin Blanc	Riesling
Sweetbreads	Torrontés	Viognier
Taramasalata	Sauvignon Blanc	Pinot Blanc
Thai Crabcakes	Pinot Noir	Oaked Chardonnay
Thai Fishcakes	Pinot Noir	Oaked Chardonnay
Tiger Prawns	Gewürztraminer	Riesling
Tomato & Basil Soup	Oaked Chardonnay	Pinot Blanc
Tomato & Mozzarella Salad	Pinot Grigio	Pinot Blanc
Tomato Soup	Viognier	Nebbiolo
Tostada Chips	Sauvignon Blanc	Riesling
Tuna Niçoise Salad	Oaked Chardonnay	Sauvignon Blanc
Vegetable Soup	Viognier	Nebbiolo
Vegetable Tempura	Riesling	Gewürztraminer
Veggie & Smoked Cheese Quesadillas	Riesling	Oaked Chardonnay
Welsh Rarebit	Syrah	Merlot
Whitebait	Melon de Bourgogne	Unoaked Chardonnay
Wild Mushroom Risotto	Syrah	Nebbiolo
Wood Pigeon	Pinot Noir	Nebbiolo

Appendix 2: Food and Wine: Main Courses

Food	Recommendation	Second Recommendation
Asian Dishes	Gewürztraminer	Riesling
Balsamic Chicken Salad	Gamay	Chardonnay
BBQ Chicken	Pinot Noir	Oaked Chardonnay
BBQ Spare Ribs	Shiraz	Sangiovese
Beef & Ale Pie	Malbec	Shiraz
Beef & Black Bean Sauce	Zinfandel	Syrah
Beef & Mushroom Pie	Malbec	Syrah
Beef & Mushroom Stroganoff	Malbec	Syrah
Beef Bourguignon	Syrah	Malbec
Beef Chow Mein	Zinfandel	Tempranillo
Beef Kebab	Malbec	Merlot
Beef Madras	Shiraz	Malbec
Beef with Black Pepper Sauce	Malbec	Zinfandel
Beef Burger	Malbec	Cabernet Sauvignon
Bubble and Squeak	Gamay	Tempranillo
Cajun Chicken	Pinot Noir	Malbec
Cajun Spiced Tuna	Gewürztraminer	Oaked Chardonnay
Calf's Liver	Malbec	Zinfandel
Cheddar Ploughman's	Gamay	Malbec
Cheeseburger	Malbec	Zinfandel
Chicken & Bacon Salad	Pinot Noir	Zinfandel
Chicken & Cashew Nuts in Yellow Bean Sauce	Pinot Noir	Oaked Chardonnay
Chicken & Green Pepper with Black Bean Sauce	Oaked Chardonnay	Zinfandel
Chicken & Mushroom Pie	Grenache	Malbec
Chicken Balti	Riesling	Gewürztraminer
Chicken Bhuna	Riesling	Sauvignon Blanc

Food	Recommendation	Second Recommendation
Chicken Biryani	Riesling	Gewürztraminer
Chicken Burger	Oaked Chardonnay	Shiraz
Chicken Casserole	Grenache	Syrah
Chicken Chasseur	Oaked Chardonnay	Malbec
Chicken Chow Mein	Riesling	Gewürztraminer
Chicken Club Sandwich	Pinot Noir	Oaked Chardonnay
Chicken Cordon Bleu	Oaked Chardonnay	Pinot Noir
Chicken Escalope	Oaked Chardonnay	Pinot Noir
Chicken Fajitas	Gewürztraminer	Riesling
Chicken in White-Wine Sauce	Chardonnay	Pinot Noir
Chicken Jalfrezi	Gewürztraminer	Sauvignon Blanc
Chicken Kebab	Gamay	Sangiovese
Chicken Kiev	Pinot Noir	Oaked Chardonnay
Chicken Korma	Merlot	Unoaked Chardonnay
Chicken Madras	Riesling	Gewürztraminer
Chicken Pasanda	Sauvignon Blanc	Riesling
Chicken Pizza	Oaked Chardonnay	Sangiovese
Chicken Risotto	Oaked Chardonnay	Sauvignon Blanc
Chicken Rogan Josh	Riesling	Sangiovese
Chicken Saag	Riesling	Gewürztraminer
Chicken Salad	Gamay	Oaked Chardonnay
Chicken Stir-Fry	Riesling	Sauvignon Blanc
Chicken Tikka Masala	Gewürztraminer	Riesling
Chicken with Chilli Sauce	Riesling	Gewürztraminer
Chicken with Red Wine Sauce	Pinot Noir	Nebbiolo
Chilli con Carne	Gewürztraminer	Riesling
Chinese Dishes	Gewürztraminer	Chenin Blanc
Chump of Lamb Hotpot	Grenache	Cabernet
Coq au Vin	Pinot Noir	Merlot
Cottage Pie	Malbec	Merlot
Crispy Aromatic Duck	Pinot Noir	Tempranillo
Curried Seafood	Riesling	Gewürztraminer

177

Food	Recommendation	Second Recommendation
Dorada Fillets	Pinot Noir	Oaked Chardonnay
Dover Sole	Pinot Noir	Oaked Chardonnay
Duck L'Orange	Pinot Noir	Tempranillo
Duck with Lemon Sauce	Riesling	Tempranillo
Entrecote Chasseur	Malbec	Tempranillo
Feta & Roasted Vegetable Salad	Oaked Chardonnay	Viognier
Fillet of Venison	Syrah	Tempranillo
Fillet Steak	Cabernet	Malbec
Fish & Chips	Oaked Chardonnay	Sauvignon Blanc
Fish Pie	Pinot Noir	Oaked Chardonnay
Game Terrine	Pinot Noir	Gamay
Gammon Steak	Merlot	Malbec
Goat's Cheese Brûlée	Sauvignon Blanc	Unoaked Chardonnay
Goat's Cheese Salad	Sauvignon Blanc	Oaked Chardonnay
Grilled Halloumi & Cherry Tomato Cassoulet	Pinot Grigio	Viognier
Grilled Red Snapper	Pinot Noir	Oaked Chardonnay
Grilled Veal	Merlot	Tempranillo
Haddock & Spring Onion Fishcake	Tempranillo	Oaked Chardonnay
Halibut Steak	Pinot Noir	Oaked Chardonnay
Halloumi & Couscous Salad	Tempranillo	Oaked Chardonnay
Ham & Eggs	Pinot Noir	Tempranillo
Ham & Mushroom Pizza	Sangiovese	Barbera
Ham & Pineapple Pizza	Unoaked Chardonnay	Barbera
Ham Hock & Pea Risotto	Merlot	Oaked Chardonnay
Herb Crusted Rack of Lamb	Cabernet	Merlot
King Prawn Curry	Riesling	Sauvignon Blanc
Kung Po Chicken	Riesling	Gewürztraminer
Kung Po Prawns	Riesling	Gewürztraminer
Lamb Balti	Shiraz	Tempranillo
Lamb Bhuna	Shiraz	Cabernet
Lamb Biryani	Merlot	Malbec
Lamb Chops	Cabernet	Malbec

Food	Recommendation	Second Recommendation
Lamb Cutlets	Cabernet	Malbec
Lamb Jalfrezi	Shiraz	Tempranillo
Lamb Korma	Merlot	Malbec
Lamb Madras	Gewürztraminer	Shiraz
Lamb Moussaka	Sangiovese	Merlot
Lamb Pasanda	Merlot	Shiraz
Lamb Rogan Josh	Merlot	Shiraz
Lamb Saag	Gewürztraminer	Shiraz
Lamb Shank	Cabernet	Merlot
Lamb Tagine	Grenache	Syrah
Lamb Tikka Masala	Merlot	Malbec
Lasagne	Malbec	Cabernet
Leek & Blue Cheese Risotto	Pinot Grigio	Merlot
Lemon Chicken	Pinot Noir	Oaked Chardonnay
Liver and Bacon	Syrah	Malbec
Lobster	Oaked Chardonnay	Pinot Noir
Macaroni Cheese	Sangiovese	Barbera
Margarita Pizza	Pinot Grigio	Pinot Blanc
Meatballs	Malbec	Cabernet
Mexican Dishes	Barbera	Cabernet Franc
Mixed Grill	Shiraz	Malbec
Moussaka	Sangiovese	Nebbiolo
Mushroom & Asparagus Risotto	Pinot Grigio	Sauvignon Blanc
Mushroom Chow Mein	Riesling	Gewürztraminer
Mushroom Stroganoff	Shiraz	Malbec
Mushroom Tarte Tatin	Sangiovese	Shiraz
Mustard Glazed Gammon	Zinfandel	Grenache
Nut Roast	Merlot	Malbec
Oriental Duck Spring Roll	Pinot Noir	Gamay
Pad Thai	Riesling	Sauvignon Blanc
Penne with Mushrooms & Pesto	Sangiovese	Barbera
Pepper Steak	Zinfandel	Malbec

Food	Recommendation	Second Recommendation
Pepperoni Pizza	Zinfandel	Sangiovese
Pheasant Breasts Braised in Cider	Pinot Noir	Merlot
Pigeon Pie	Pinot Noir	Syrah
Pineapple Pork with Noodles	Tempranillo	Pinot Noir
Piquant Lamb	Cabernet Sauvignon	Merlot
Piri Piri Beef	Malbec	Cabernet
Piri Piri Chicken	Sangiovese	Tempranillo
Pizza	Barbaresco	Barolo
Polenta Dishes	Corvina	Nebbiolo
Polenta with Chargrilled Vegetables & Halloumi	Grenache	Oaked Chardonnay
Pork alla Genovese	Pinot Noir	Malbec
Pork Chops	Merlot	Malbec
Pork Kiev with Caramelised Apples	Pinot Noir	Grenache
Pork Medallions with Cider	Pinot Noir	Chardonnay
Pork Stuffed with Pears and Blackberries	Pinot Noir	Malbec
Pork Tenderloin with Sage	Pinot Noir	Gamay
Potato Gnocchi	Sangiovese	Barbera
Prawn Risotto	Oaked Chardonnay	Viognier
Quail Skewers	Pinot Noir	Cabernet Franc
Quiche Lorraine	Pinot Noir	Gamay
Rabbit and Pearl Barley Stew	Shiraz	Grenache
Rack of Lamb	Cabernet	Malbec
Ravioli	Sangiovese	Shiraz
Rib Eye Steak	Malbec	Cabernet
Roast Beef	Malbec	Cabernet
Roast Chicken	Pinot Noir	Oaked Chardonnay
Roast Duck with Taro	Pinot Noir	Syrah
Roast Gammon	Merlot	Malbec
Roast Goose	Cabernet Sauvignon	Zinfandel
Roast Guinea Fowl	Pinot Noir	Zinfandel

Food	Recommendation	Second Recommendation
Roast Lamb	Cabernet	Malbec
Roast Partridge	Pinot Noir	Gamay
Roast Pork	Cabernet	Syrah
Roast Turkey	Pinot Noir	Oaked Chardonnay
Roast Duck Breast	Pinot Noir	Oaked Chardonnay
Roast Skate	Oaked Chardonnay	Sauvignon Blanc
Rump Steak	Malbec	Cabernet
Salad of Pigeon and Caramelised Leeks	Grenache	Syrah
Salmon Fillet	Pinot Noir	Oaked Chardonnay
Salmon Fishcakes	Pinot Noir	Oaked Chardonnay
Salmon Salad	Pinot Noir	Oaked Chardonnay
Sausages & Mash	Malbec	Syrah
Scampi & Chips	Oaked Chardonnay	Chenin Blanc
Scampi Provençale	Sauvignon Blanc	Chenin Blanc
Seabass Fillet	Pinot Noir	Oaked Chardonnay
Seafood Paella	Sauvignon Blanc	Melon de Bourgogne
Seafood Pasta	Sangiovese	Sauvignon Blanc
Seafood Platter	Champagne	Chardonnay
Seared Breast of Wood Pigeon	Syrah	Tempranillo
Seared King Scallops	Pinot Noir	Sauvignon Blanc
Seared Tuna Loin	Oaked Chardonnay	Pinot Noir
Shepherd's Pie	Grenache	Sangiovese
Shish Kebab	Syrah	Tempranillo
Shredded Chilli Beef	Riesling	Gewürztraminer
Shredded Chilli Chicken	Riesling	Gewürztraminer
Singapore Noodles	Riesling	Gewürztraminer
Sirloin Steak	Malbec	Cabernet
Slow-Roast Ginger Pork	Gamay	Tempranillo
Smoked Haddock Hash	Pinot Noir	Oaked Chardonnay
Smoked Salmon Ravioli	Sangiovese	Barbera
Spaghetti Bolognese	Sangiovese	Nebbiolo
Spaghetti Carbonara	Sangiovese	Nebbiolo

Food	Recommendation	Second Recommendation
Spice Crusted Duck with Black Pepper Risotto	Pinot Noir	Zinfandel
Spicy Enchiladas	Malbec	Gewürztraminer
Spicy Tomato Linguine	Pinot Grigio	Sangiovese
Spring Lamb with Spinach	Cabernet Sauvignon	Merlot
Steak Diane	Malbec	Cabernet
Steak Fajitas	Malbec	Tempranillo
Stilton & Broccoli Bake	Oaked Chardonnay	Merlot
Stuffed Mushrooms	Viognier	Merlot
Stuffed Pheasant Breast	Pinot Noir	Syrah
Stuffed Saddle of Rabbit	Zinfandel	Malbec
Surf & Turf	Pinot Noir	Malbec
Sushi	Chenin Blanc	Riesling
Sweet & Sour Chicken	Gewürztraminer	Riesling
Sweet & Sour Pork	Gewürztraminer	Riesling
Sweet & Sour Prawns	Gewürztraminer	Riesling
Sweet Potato & Aubergine Curry	Gewürztraminer	Riesling
Swordfish Milanese	Pinot Noir	Sauvignon Blanc
Szechuan Beef	Gewürztraminer	Riesling
Szechuan Chicken	Gewürztraminer	Riesling
Szechuan Pork	Gewürztraminer	Riesling
Thai Dishes	Riesling	Pinotage
Thai Green Chicken Curry	Sauvignon Blanc	Riesling
Thai Red Chicken Curry	Gewürztraminer	Riesling
Thai Red King Prawn Curry	Gewürztraminer	Riesling
Thai Yellow Chicken Curry	Gewürztraminer	Riesling
Tiger Prawn Stir-Fry	Gewürztraminer	Riesling
Tomato & Basil Penne	Sangiovese	Barbera
Trout Almondine	Pinot Noir	Oaked Chardonnay
Tuna Steak	Oaked Chardonnay	Viognier
Turkey, Gammon & Mushroom Pie	Cabernet	Syrah
Veal Aurora	Merlot	Malbec

Food	Recommendation	Second Recommendation
Veal Risotto	Malbec	Merlot
Vegetable Balti	Riesling	Gewürztraminer
Vegetable Bhuna	Riesling	Gewürztraminer
Vegetable Biryani	Riesling	Gewürztraminer
Vegetable Burrito	Sauvignon Blanc	Riesling
Vegetable Chilli	Riesling	Gewürztraminer
Vegetable Chow Mein	Riesling	Sauvignon Blanc
Vegetable Curry	Riesling	Gewürztraminer
Vegetable Fajitas	Gewürztraminer	Riesling
Vegetable Jalfrezi	Gewürztraminer	Riesling
Vegetable Korma	Sauvignon Blanc	Riesling
Vegetable Lasagne	Sangiovese	Merlot
Vegetable Madras	Gewürztraminer	Riesling
Vegetable Moussaka	Syrah	Merlot
Vegetable Pasanda	Gewürztraminer	Riesling
Vegetable Risotto	Merlot	Pinot Noir
Vegetable Rogan Josh	Gewürztraminer	Riesling
Vegetable Saag	Gewürztraminer	Riesling
Vegetable Stir-Fry	Sauvignon Blanc	Riesling
Vegetable Tikka Masala	Gewürztraminer	Riesling
Vegetarian Pizza	Gamay	Sangiovese
Veggie Burger	Malbec	Merlot